YUGOSLAVIA

1988/1989 Edition

By the staff of Berlitz Guides
A Macmillan Company

How to use our guide

These 256 pages cover the **highlights of Yugoslavia,** grouped by geographical region. Although not exhaustive, our selection of sights will enable you to make the best of your trip.

The **sights** to see are contained between pages 38 and 191. Those most highly recommended are pinpointed by the Berlitz traveller symbol.

The **Where to Go** section on page 34 will help you plan your visit according to the time available.

For **general background** see the sections Yugoslavia and the Yugoslavs (p. 8), Facts and Figures (p. 18), History (p. 19) and Historical Landmarks (p. 33).

Entertainment and **activities** (including eating out) are described between pages 192 and 211.

The **practical information,** hints and tips you will need before and during your trip begin on page 212. This section is arranged alphabetically with a list of contents for easy reference.

The **map section** at the back of the book (pp. 242–252) will help you find your way around and locate the principal sights.

Finally, if there is anything you cannot find, look in the complete **index** (pp. 253–256).

CONTENTS

CONTENTS

Cover photo: Primošten, Dalmatian coast

4

Text:	Ken Bernstein with Madge Tomašević and Karin Radovanović
Photography:	Claude Huber cover, pp. 43, 44, 45, 49, 51, 57, 59, 63, 64, 67, 68, 70, 72, 73, 74, 75, 76, 77, 81, 83, 85, 86, 99, 101, 103, 107, 134, 160, 195, 207 Erling Mandelmann; pp. 97, 105, 113, 122 Daniel Vittet; p. 136 Hans Rudolf Uthoff.
Layout:	Doris Haldemann
Cartography:	🌀 Falk-Verlag, Hamburg p. 27 Max Thommen

Acknowledgements
We would like to thank Zvonimir Petek, Director of the Yugoslavian National Tourist Office in Zurich, for his help in the preparation of this guide. We are very grateful to Dragiča Krstić and Milka Popović of the Yugoslavian National Tourist Office in Belgrade. Our appreciation also goes to Naum Dimitrijević and Sara Crowgey for their valuable contribution.

Found an error or an omission in this Berlitz Guide? Or a change or new feature we should know about? Our editor would be happy to hear from you, and a postcard would do. Be sure to include your name and address, since in appreciation for a useful suggestion, we'd like to send you a free travel guide.

Although we make every effort to ensure the accuracy of all the information in this book, changes occur incessantly. We cannot therefore take responsibility for facts, prices, addresses and circumstances in general that are constantly subject to alteration.

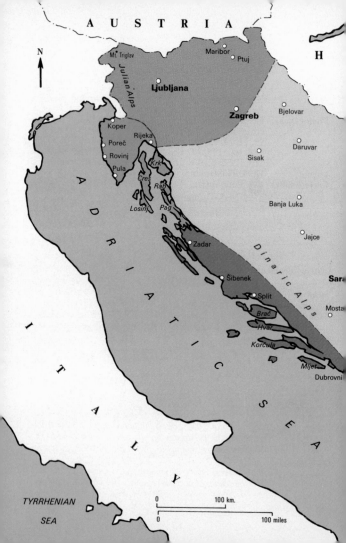

H U N G A R Y

Subotica

Novi Sad

ovar

Sabac

BELGRADE

R U M A N I A

Djerdap

Kraljevo

Studenica

Sopoćani Novi Pazar

Niš

Leskovac

Priština

ograd

Peć

Dečani

Gračanica

B U L G A R I A

ake Skadar

Prizren

Ulcinj

A L B A N I A

Tetovo

Skopje

Ohrid

Lake Ohrid

Bitola

Lake Prespa

G R E E C E

YUGOSLAVIA AND THE YUGOSLAVS

Poised between east and west, Yugoslavia offers a sampling of Europe's best: picture-book cities and ancient ruins, romantic rivers and lakes, Alpine ski slopes and Adriatic beaches.

Beyond these worthy tourist sights hides a heady helping of less predictable attractions: stark karst mountains riddled with canyons and caves; skylines of castles, church steeples and minarets; bear hunting and bare sunbathing; and the hospitable people themselves. Ranging from blond to swarthy, they're a cross-section of Europe and beyond.

You may well be braced for something different. After all, this

is the Balkans, notorious powder-keg and all that. Even the map sizzles with suggestions of international intrigue: *Bosnia! Montenegro! Sarajevo! Rijeka!* And the imagination works overtime on place-names like *Niš, Bled, Krk* and *Ptuj,* as concise as cavemen's grunts.

You don't have to go far in Yugoslavia to find the exotic. Just wade into the crowd at the nearest street market, a seething smorgasbord of nationalities, costumes and delicacies and a hubbub of languages. Consider the profusion of cathedrals, monasteries and mosques: most Yugoslavs are Orthodox or Catholic, but the country also has Europe's

700 years and 500 miles separate Ohrid church, modern Slovenia.

largest Muslim community. And everywhere you'll be surrounded by a fascinating modern phenomenon, a one-of-a-kind social system.

"Workers' self-management" is the guiding principle of contemporary Yugoslavian society. You'll have plenty of opportunities to see this version of socialism in action—in your hotel, in shops and offices. (But small, privately owned businesses are also prospering.) Politically and ideologically, the League of Communists of Yugoslavia, with more than two million members, plays a leading role.

If all this striving for a classless society conjures up frenzied sloganeering, hard-nosed bureaucrats, overbearing guides and travel restrictions, you're thinking of the wrong country. Nonconformist Yugoslavia, where the non-aligned movement started, extends a friendly hand to east and west alike. Foreign tourists receive an unqualified welcome; you're invited to see virtually everything, everywhere—on your own. Everything including the workings, sometimes less than perfect, of Yugoslavian society.

When it comes to melting-pots, no country in Europe can top the complexity of Yugoslavia's ethnic mix. Although scarcely bigger than Britain or West Germany, Yugoslavia is made up of four principal nationalities plus a couple of dozen minority groups enjoying certain rights of autonomy. The population of nearly 23 million writes in two different alphabets, Latin and Cyrillic, and speaks three main languages (four if you count Serbo-Croatian as a pair). Yugoslavs also express themselves in a gaggle of peripheral tongues as arcane as Albanian and Ruthenian. As in the UN, delegates to the National Assembly wear earphones for simultaneous translations of the speeches.

You aren't likely to need an interpreter to make yourself understood. English is much studied in the schools nowadays; if that fails, you might make a stab at German or Italian, the traditional international languages here.

With its entry into the ranks of the superpowers of European tourism, Yugoslavia has inevitably become more cosmopolitan. Another sophisticating factor is the exodus of Yugoslavian "guest-workers" to the capitalist world. This brain-and-brawn drain has put *ćevapčići* on the menus of West Berlin and Zurich. More importantly, it has eased Yugoslavia's unemployment problem and provided hard currency for the chronically besieged balance of payments.

Dubrovnik serenade: choristers make music in a living museum.

The geographical features of Yugoslavia are as diverse as the ethnic mosaic. The country spreads from north-west to south-east; if you stare at the map long enough, Yugoslavia's shape might blearily resemble a plunging hippopotamus. Offshoots of the Alps run down the beast's back, the heart of the nation.

This very hilly country rises into forested mountains imposing enough to have haunted many an invader, and Yugoslavia has been overrun by the best and worst of them. Forbidding but beautiful Montenegro (meaning "black mountain") is that sort of redoubt, but the country's summit rises far to the north-west: Mount Triglav—altitude 2,864 metres or 9,397 feet—in Slovenia's skiable Julian Alps.

Paralleling the Adriatic coast, the karst region's steep white limestone mountains are pierced by gorges, caves and underground rivers. Happily, the barrenness is relieved by splashes of wild flowers and compact valleys farmers have turned into oases. The science of geology has appropriated the term "karst" (*krš,* tersely, in the original Serbo-Croatian) to describe any landscape in the world formed by the dramatic interaction of rainwater and limestone.

Northern Yugoslavia, and specifically the sweeping Pannonian Plain, is watered by the mighty

Danube, Europe's second-largest river (after the Volga). You can swim in it, or go fishing, or take an excursion. Stretches of three other Yugoslavian rivers are also navigable, and there are some 250 lakes.

The other decisive liquid asset is the Adriatic Sea, which laps more than 2,000 kilometres (1,200 miles) of intricately indented coastline. The locals are quick to pad these statistics, legitimate-

Serbian hayride: oxen still supply the power down on the farm.

ly enough, by tacking on the circumferences of the country's countless Adriatic islands. They contribute another 4,000-odd kilometres (2,500 miles) of beaches. All of this makes the most of a seashore that in reality measures only 628 kilometres (389 miles) from end to end, as the dolphin swims.

The Adriatic itself, a narrow subsidiary of the Mediterranean, is so transparent it's unfair to the fish. It can be as calm as a pond, or as tricky as the winds that converge on it. The lovely coastline, with its rocky inlets, pebbly coves and sandy beaches, was all but undiscovered until recent years. The adventurous tourists who headed east to escape crowds and commercialization started an irresistible tide. But by then the errors and excesses of Europe's overexploited Costas could be taken into account; in Yugoslavia, reason and good taste have survived the tourist revolution.

Like the topography, Yugoslavia's climate is a blend of continental and Mediterranean, supporting mountain pines and tropical palms. In winter, even as people on the coast sip coffee and brandy at their outdoor cafés, the mercury can tumble to well below freezing point in the mountains or the northern plain. Summers are hot, sometimes cruelly so, in the interior and hot and dry along the coast. Everyone is highly conscious of the winds, which blow hot and cold and sometimes ill. The wind called *jugo,* for instance, means rain, while the *maestral* brings relief from a heat wave. The dreaded *bura* is a cold, violent nor'easter.

This land has been making its mark on civilization, and vice versa, since the Stone Age. But the real founders of Yugoslavia didn't arrive on the scene until late in the 6th century, long after a wealth of Roman monuments had been installed. It took another 1,300-odd years before the state called Yugoslavia was proclaimed. The last nuances of the country's present-day boundaries were finally settled in 1954.

"Yugoslav" means South Slav. The South Slavs are the sunny-side branch of Europe's biggest ethnic family, whose cousins include Russians, Ukrainians and Poles. The Slavs apparently moved into the area with no particular master plan. They were fleeing southwards ahead of plundering hordes of Avar nomads.

The South Slavs consisted primarily of three groups: the Croats, the Serbs and the Slovenes. Today these nationalities account for a majority of the Yugoslavian population. Other nationalities, with their varied costumes, cuisines and languages, add a lot of spice to the Slavic stew. Among the more sizable groups are Bosnian Muslims, Macedonians, Albanians and Montenegrins. Of course, the land and the people have undergone many drastic changes since the Slavs settled down, for instance during four centuries of Turkish occupation. The vicissitudes are reflected in the weather-beaten stones, the works of art, and the faces themselves.

If you have a preconception about the Yugoslavs, it's probably half right. You may think of them as Mediterranean people, but you're in for a blond-haired surprise in the north, where the plump faces are pale and the eyes as cool as a fjord. Yet in southern parts you'll be surrounded by sun-browned faces and dark, flashing eyes, and drooping moustaches the men wear as haughtily as medals. In between, the people come in all varieties.

Yugoslavs themselves have their own stereotypes, and as everywhere else a particle of truth usually lurks behind a cliché. They say Serbs are a bit rustic but good-hearted, Dalmatian lads are Don Juans, Montenegrins disdainful of work, and Slovenes stingy. Bosnians are the butts of the equivalent of silly Irish jokes. Clearly, in a country so kaleidoscopic, there's simply no such thing as a typical Yugoslav.

But make your own judgments. See the people in their native environment, driving tractors or oxen, tending their vines or mending fishing nets. Be jostled in the Mediterranean-style markets, where the sellers are proud of their radishes, onions, cherries and strawberries, and let you know it. Join the crowds in the *korzo,* the ritual promenade of early evening, supervised by the village elders at their café tables. This inescapable phenomenon, a Mediterranean tradition, is part of daily life in towns all over the country, even far from the sea.

Any A to Z survey of Yugoslavia's attractions starts at the seaside—the Adriatic. (This happy alphabetical accident doesn't happen in Serbo-Croatian, though; the Adriatic's local name is *Jadransko more.*) The coast, with its highly developed network of hotels and services, is the destination of more than three-fourths of all tourists. They can choose from a bounty of bays and beaches for all tastes. But the Adriatic offers far more than a swim and a sun-tan. Over many centuries, man has embellished the coast with citadels of stone that might have been transplanted from Venice or Constantinople. So a seaside holiday here, on the mainland or the isles, can include a cultural dimension.

B is for Belgrade, standing at the confluence of the River Danube and another Yugoslavian lifeline, the Sava. The strategic importance of the site has been recognized for thousands of years. After all the battles for control of Belgrade, not much of profound historical interest is still standing; the museums, though, are worthwhile. In the sweltering Serbian summer the outdoor cafés add more parasols, tables and chairs, leaving little room for pedestrians, but no matter. For a capital city it's all very relaxed.

C (pronounced tseh) calls to mind Cetinje, a one-time capital hidden away in the mountains. A charming exercise in nostalgia, this storybook town with its quaint palaces and defunct embassies served as the seat of the valiant Montenegrin kingdom until 1918.

D doubtless means Dubrovnik, back on the coast, a precious monument, one of the great

15

sights of the world. Mighty stone walls and urbane diplomacy assured the freedom of this medieval city-state. With its palaces, churches and majestic plazas, it looks like a scaled-down Venice with car-less streets instead of canals.

And so on through a roll-call of historic towns, and islands as pithily named as Hvar, Pag and Rab, winding up in the alphabetical end-zone at Zagreb, the culture-minded capital of Croatia. This go-ahead city of parks and squares takes itself seriously... deservedly.

The dedicated, or even moderately inquisitive, tourist will be exhausted long before running out of sightseeing possibilities, from Roman ruins to medieval monasteries to modern art. And between excursions, the what-to-do menu is as comprehensive as the small print in an insurance policy. The seaside has its obvious activities—swimming, snorkelling, sailing and water-skiing, for instance. Ashore there is tennis (a commonplace at resort hotels) and golf (but on a small scale). The mountains are for hiking, climbing and skiing (though the après-ski life isn't as elaborate as in some neighbouring countries). Or try the bird-watching or hunting (wild boar abound).

Whether or not anything ails you, you can "take a cure" at one of Yugoslavia's relaxing spas—or drink the therapeutic waters by the bottle, anywhere. Or "take it off" at a nudist camp; Yugoslavia outstrips just about every other country in what is formally called "naturism". The trend was set in 1936 on the island of Rab, where King Edward VIII is said to have pioneered royal skinny-dipping.

Shopping, a high-priority activity for many tourists, can be pursued on all levels in Yugoslavia, from modern department stores and fashion boutiques to bazaars exuding eastern colour. The "best buys" range from arts and crafts to sportswear and skis.

An even more obligatory tourist pursuit: experiencing the country's ethnic spectrum through the foods of the different regions. The possibilities are as varied as goulash, strudel and Turkish delight; and the seafood couldn't be better. The unaffected wine is remarkably good and inexpensive. After dinner, the nightlife runs to folklore or a disco beat, watching an outdoor movie or just admiring the way the moon lights a medieval palace or cathedral.

History, of course, surrounds you in Yugoslavia. For that matter, even the prices will remind you of the Good Old Days.

One of a kind: the Multi-coloured Mosque in Tetovo, Macedonia.

FACTS AND FIGURES

Geography: With an area of 255,804 square kilometres (98,766 square miles), Yugoslavia is about the size of Wyoming or West Germany. It borders countries of many political complexions: Italy, Austria, Hungary, Romania, Bulgaria, Greece and Albania. The length of Yugoslavia's Adriatic coastline is reckoned at 2,092 kilometres (1,299 miles), but adding the circumference of the country's approximately 1,000 islands and islets brings the total to 6,116 kilometres (3,798 miles). The highest point in this mountainous country is Mt. Triglav, reaching 2,864 metres (9,397 feet). The principal river, the Sava, is 945 kilometres (587 miles) long; the Danube *(Dunav* in Serbo-Croatian) flows through Yugoslavia for 588 kilometres (365 miles). There are some 250 lakes.

Population: Nearly 23 million. Principal ethnic groups: Serbs 36%, Croats 20%, Bosnian Muslims 9%, Slovenes 8%, Macedonians 6%, Albanians 8%, Montenegrins 3%, Hungarians 2%.

Capital: Belgrade *(Beograd)*, population around 1,500,000.

Major cities: Zagreb (more than one million), Skopje (500,000), Sarajevo (450,000), Ljubljana (300,000).

Government: Federal socialist republic uniting six republics (Bosnia-Hercegovina, Croatia, Macedonia, Montenegro, Serbia, Slovenia) and the autonomous provinces of Kosovo and Vojvodina. Head of state: president rotating within a collective presidency, with one representative from each republic and autonomous province plus the president of the League of Communists. Executive: Federal Executive Council. Legislature: bicameral Assembly.

Religion: About 50 different churches and sects are represented, with Christians the great majority. Largest single religion: Orthodox, followed by Roman Catholic. Muslims comprise more than ten per cent of the population.

Language: Serbo-Croatian, Slovenian and Macedonian are the majority languages; many other languages are also spoken by national minorities.

HISTORY

Since ancient times Yugoslavia has often played, if not always enjoyed, the role of a buffer between east and west.

Living in a gateway has meant meeting the most interesting people, but the buffer zone has repeatedly been used as a doormat. Plunderers in transit have been passing this way for thousands of years and doing their worst before moving on to their original target. Some of the warriors stayed long enough to change the face of the nation.

Oddly, for a land so ancient, the country called Yugoslavia has existed only since 1918. Its name became official even more recently. And the present borders weren't delineated until after World War II.

Yugoslavian archaeologists can take you back to the Stone Age. The remains of a prehistoric man unearthed at Krapina in Croatia are supposed to be 40,000 years old, plus or minus a few millenia. And less venerable hoards of cave men's relics—pottery and tools—have been found elsewhere in the country.

Moving forward to a more recent prehistoric era: plentiful discoveries at Lepenski Vir, on the Danube east of Belgrade, show one of Europe's earliest civilizations apparently thriving around 6000 B.C.

History itself begins with the ancient Greeks. Around the 5th century B.C. Greek travellers took note of two primitive peoples inhabiting the area: the Illyrians and the Thracians. Both tribes were described as fierce and warlike, not exactly disadvantages in those dog-eat-dog days.

The Greeks established trading stations on the Dalmatian coast (at Split and Trogir, for instance) and nearby islands (Hvar and Korčula). The merchants were in it for the profit, not for conquest or colonial grandeur, so they largely ignored life beyond the Adriatic coast. Few tangible reminders are left to document the Greek era here.

The Roman Conquest

By the 3rd century B.C. the Illyrians were organized in a kingdom, its capital situated in what is now Albania. The Romans, just across the narrow sea in Italy, complained that Illyrian pirates were harrassing their shipping. It was only a matter of a couple of tense centuries before Rome had conquered the upstart kingdom, thenceforth known as the province of Illyricum. Under Roman rule the diverse territory now known as Yugoslavia was united for the first time. The second time came 1,500 years later.

For nearly three centuries the people enjoyed the customary benefits of Roman civilization—

19

HISTORY

A far corner of 1st-century Rome: the amphitheatre in Pula, Istria.

good roads, bread and circuses. Of course the country's strategic position was important to Rome for commercial and military purposes. And the empire exploited the local minerals.

As for those circuses, featuring animal acts for the bloodthirsty but no clowns for the children, one of Rome's biggest amphitheatres was built in Pula. Another mammoth souvenir of the era, which you can also explore, is the 3rd-century Diocletian's Palace at Split. The Emperor Diocletian (285–305), soldier, statesman and inventor of wage and price controls, was one of a surprising total of five Illyrians who climbed to the top of Rome's slippery political ladder.

Attempting to streamline the bureaucracy, Diocletian decentralized administration, splitting the empire into an eastern and a western part. Diocletian's dividing line is still engraved, though invisibly, on the map of Yugoslavia. It separates two cultures: Catholicism and the Latin alphabet to the west, the Orthodox Church and the Cyrillic alphabet to the east.

Slavs Move In

With the breakdown of the Roman empire, the Dark Ages unfolded precariously for every-

body except avaricious Vandals, vandalistic Avars and barbarous Huns. Among the refugees rushing to get out of the way of the aggressors were the Slavs. During the 6th and 7th centuries they found sanctuary in Illyria, where they put down deep roots.

The South Slavs were made up of three tribes: the Slovenes, the Serbs and the Croats. As often as not they fought among themselves, but common enemies inspired renewed feelings of kinship. Like long-lost friends, their histories diverge, then overlap, then drift apart, finally coinciding in modern times. Their destinies also intersect the sinuous lifelines of the others in the complicated cast of characters making up Yugoslavia. Among the principals: the Bosnians, Macedonians and Montenegrins.

During more than a thousand years from the arrival of the Slavs to the end of the long, daunting Ottoman occupation (the great national trauma), a few names and events stand out—starting with two monks from Macedonia who were to become saints. Cyril and his brother Methodius, 9th-century missionaries to the Slavs, translated the Bible into Slavic. To suit the sounds of the language they devised an alphabet, later known as Cyrillic in honour of the younger brother, and laid the foundations for a unified South Slav culture.

Serbia's Golden Age

For several centuries after they arrived in the Balkans, the Serbs fought each other as furiously as they would fight their neighbours later on. Princes vied for power in a state of confusion remarkable even by local standards. At last unity corralled the Serbs with the establishment of the Nemanja dynasty in the 12th century. The high-point of the era, in which the Serbian Orthodox Church was established, was the career of Stefan Dušan (1331–55). This ambitious tsar pushed Serbia's borders out as far as Albania, promulgated a code of laws, and rescued the balance of payments. A golden age of art flourished in the Serbian monasteries, their walls covered from floor to ceiling with heavenly frescoes.

Trouble, though, came soon enough. In 1389 the Serbs and their allies dug in to face the irresistible Turkish tide of Islam. The fateful battle, on the plain of Kosovo, all but wiped out the Christian army. Serbian Prince Lazar lost his head, literally, as the scimitar-swishing Turks took control of the battlefield. Nor was it a romp for the Turks, whose chief, Sultan Murad I, also perished in the fray. The Kosovo disaster gave the Turks the mo-

Fervent faith inspired the golden age of Orthodox art in Serbia.

momentum to overrun Europe as far north as Vienna; the Serbs were inspired to guerilla war or the despair of emigration.

Through the long years of Ottoman domination, the Serbs preserved their identity and their faith. Repeated rebellions eventually led to the creation of the autonomous principality of Serbia in 1830. Finally, in 1878, Serbia became an independent state.

Medieval Croatia

While Serbia had embraced the eastern branch of Christianity, Croatia was allied with its own Adriatic neighbours and the Church of Rome. By the 10th century Croats had overcome domestic quarrels and foreign masters to form an independent country. But soon an epidemic of domestic unrest prompted feuding Croatian leaders to ask the

King of Hungary to take charge. The Magyar connection endured almost without interruption until modern times.

Landlocked Hungary understandably cast a covetous eye at Dalmatia, covering much of coastal Croatia and beyond. To achieve this generous outlet to the sea, the Hungarians couldn't avoid a conflict of interest with the Venetians, whose sea routes were vulnerable to pirates, self-employed or official. Inevitably, armed conflict ensued. One historian counted 21 wars between Venice and Hungary in the Middle Ages. Venice gradually con-

Worshippers cover their heads in Priština mosque and Zagreb shrine.

solidated its hold on what has been called "a Slavonic land with an Italian fringe". The Venetian influence on the region's art was all for the good, as witness the many noble churches, cathedrals and palaces.

Impregnable Montenegro

At one time, links between Venice and Montenegro were close and cordial. In fact the name, Montenegro, can be traced back to the Venetian dialect translation of Black Mountain, or Crna Gora as the locals call it.

But Venice became ancient history when the Turkish invaders cut Montenegro's access to the sea. The sturdy mountaineers withdrew to their inhospitable redoubt, where they fought the Turks for nearly four centuries.

While all this was going on, in the 16th century Montenegro became a theocracy, a state ruled by an Orthodox bishop. Even more unconventionally, power became hereditary; since the bishops were supposed to be celibate it was their nephews who ensured the succession. The most celebrated of Montenegrin rulers was the 19th-century prince-bishop, Petar II Njegoš, not only a noted warrior, statesman and billiard player but also the national poet.

The Bosnian Heresy

Medieval religious developments in Bosnia shook the established churches, already split between east and west. Iconoclastic Bosnians abandoned the Old Testament and much of the New to join the ascetic Bogomil religion. The sect, a Balkan phenomenon, was named after a 10th-century Bulgarian priest, Bogomil (Beloved of God). In Bosnia the religion grew into a national movement uniting the nobility and the merest shepherd.

The Bogomils turned their backs on the material world as a

All in the Family

In the early 20th century the hitherto obscure principality of Montenegro won increasing recognition as an independent country, largely due to the tireless efforts of King Nikola I (and only). Even his enemies had to admire his fertile imagination in the realm of dynamic dynastic diplomacy.

He married one of his daughters to the heir to the Italian throne and another to the future king of Serbia. Four more children married into the royal families of Germany and Russia.

At first Nikola was a prince like all the previous Montenegrin rulers, but in keeping with his rising self-esteem he styled himself Royal Highness and then just plain King. He is better remembered, perhaps, as "the father-in-law of Europe".

creation of the devil. Many a Bogomil suffered persecution from Catholic and Orthodox neighbours for sticking to a heretical faith. Thus when the triumphant Turkish army arrived in the 15th century, the Bogomils welcomed their conquerors. Theologically the Bogomils found some familiar elements in Islam, and many converted to the invader's faith. Prospering under the Ottoman empire, the Bosnian capital, Sarajevo, turned into a Turkish-style boom town with mosques and monasteries, bazaars and caravanserais. To this day, the population of the republic of Bosnia-Hercegovina contains a large percentage of Muslims, who are recognized as a distinct nation within Yugoslavia.

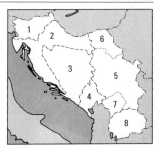

Republics and autonomous provinces of Yugoslavia: 1 Slovenia, 2 Croatia, 3 Bosnia-Hercegovina, 4 Montenegro, 5 Serbia, 6 Vojvodina, 7 Kosovo, 8 Macedonia.

Napoleon's Illyria

In the beginning of the 19th century a new occupying power, the burgeoning French empire of Napoleon, quietly seized much of the coast and additional territory inland. In the first stage, Dalmatia, which had briefly been held by Austria, was ceded to France in 1805. Napoleon soon grabbed additional lands in Croatia, Istria and beyond. With a fond look back into Roman history he grandly renamed his new colony the Illyrian Provinces. This long view was scant consolation for the citizens of the republic of Dubrovnik, who lost their independence for the first time in hundreds of years.

Taking the offensive against Napoleon, British and Austrian forces besieged Illyria by land and sea. The English occupied several of the most desirable Adriatic islands, including Hvar and Korčula. But when a beaten Napoleon abandoned Illyria, it was the Austrians who became the new masters.

For all the unpleasantness of the French interlude, there were some specific benefits, particularly in the fields of commerce and law and order. The occupation also imposed unity on Slovenes, Serbs and Croats, suggesting the possibility of a freely created, independent South Slav state.

27

It Started in Sarajevo

On a sunny summer Sunday, June 28, 1914, the heir to the Austro-Hungarian empire, Archduke Franz Ferdinand, and his wife paid a formal visit to Sarajevo. In spite of widespread resentment at foreign rule, flag-waving Bosnians lined the streets. Suddenly a bomb thrown from the crowd bounced off the archducal car and exploded in the road. The archduke was spared anything more serious than a scratch somewhere north of his handlebar moustache. But the conspiracy had only begun.

Less than an hour later, after an awkward spell of speeches at the town hall, the motorcade slowed unexpectedly. A young man emerged from the throng and fired two shots at point blank range. Both the archduke and his wife were mortally wounded.

The assassin, Gavrilo Princip, now rates as a local hero, a selfless Bosnian patriot. For a stunned Austro-Hungarian empire, it looked like an open and shut case, a Serbian plot. After a month of shock and shouting, Austria-Hungary declared war. Days later, the sparks of a provincial conflict in the Balkans blew up into the flaming horror of

In the footprints of an assassin: honouring the archduke's killer.

28

World War I, in which more than eight million troops would perish.

After heroically checking the Austro-Hungarian advance and, incidentally, winning the first Allied victory of the war, the exhausted Serbian armies retreated across the snow of the Albanian mountains to find refuge on the island of Corfu. Here the concept of a united Yugoslavia formally took shape—a declaration favouring a single nation under the Serbian crown in which all Yugoslavian peoples would enjoy complete equality.

Searching for Unity

In the years between the world wars the Yugoslavian republics seemed to confirm all the clichés about the Balkan tinderbox. Life was an endless round of discords, Byzantine manoeuverings and assassinations.

For example, in 1928 a Montenegrin deputy whipped out a revolver in the Assembly and fatally wounded three Croats, including the influential peasant leader Stephen Radić. The following year King Alexander dissolved parliament, abolished the constitution and proclaimed a royal dictatorship.

Then the country's name was changed to Yugoslavia. But nothing seemed to change the bleak situation for the economy. The world depression of the early 1930s brought unemployment to an explosive 40 per cent. There was a run on the banks. And then, in 1934, while on a state visit to France, King Alexander was assassinated by an agent working for Macedonian and Croatian separatist groups. Patriots said his last words were, "Protect Yugoslavia".

Staggered by these disasters and surrounded by the growing menace of Hitler and Mussolini, Yugoslavia tried to steer clear of Europe's approaching confrontations. But the force of external pressures silenced all the protestations of neutrality.

In March 1941, Prince Paul, the regent, went to Hitler's Berchtesgaden hideaway for a secret audience with the *Führer*. The resulting agreements pledged Yugoslavia's support for the Axis in return for the promise of Salonica (Greek Macedonia). Irate Yugoslavs sent Paul packing into exile. By popular demand the new government renounced the Axis pact, so enraging Hitler that he declared he would wipe Yugoslavia off the map. In response, all the government could do was urge everyone to remain calm and declare Belgrade, Zagreb and Ljubljana open cities.

Invasion and Resistance

April 6, 1941, Palm Sunday: without the courtesy of a declaration of war, the *Luftwaffe* bombed Belgrade. Axis troops rolled across five frontiers. Ill-prepared and betrayed, the defending armies of young King Peter capitulated within ten days. As Peter fled into exile, Germany, Italy, Bulgaria, Hungary and Albania seized slices of Yugoslavian territory; a satellite state of Croatia was formed, and Germany occupied Serbia, ruling with a government of collaborators.

But the vanquished struck back. Guerilla bands soon organized large-scale resistance activities. Initially, the communist-led partisans and royalist Chetniks under Colonel Draža Mihailović agreed to join forces against the enemy. But it soon became apparent that they were too incompatible politically to cooperate. Evidence piled up that the Chetniks were assisting the Germans in ferreting out the partisans, and by 1943 the Allies were dropping supplies only to the partisans' National Liberation Army, commanded by Josip Broz, code-name Tito.

The triumphant uphill fight of the partisans in pinning down tens of thousands of enemy troops and finally liberating their own country has been widely told. The price the Yugoslavs paid for their liberty was high—the loss of more than 1,700,000 lives.

A Republic Proclaimed

At the end of 1943, Tito was named marshal of Yugoslavia and president of the National Liberation Committee (a provisional government). As peacetime leader of a new Yugoslavia—proclaimed a socialist federal republic—he totally altered the course of his country's economic and political life.

In 1948 Yugoslavia broke with Stalin, abandoning Soviet tutelage to create a distinctive brand of socialism based on worker

Larger-than-Life Leader

The paramount Yugoslav was the seventh of 15 children of a Croatian father and a Slovenian mother. Drafted in World War I, Josip Broz was wounded and captured by the Russians. Returning to Yugoslavia as a communist, he was arrested repeatedly for his underground political activities. In 1936 Stalin's Cominform summoned him to work in Moscow. In 1937 he became secretary general of the Yugoslavian party.

After his spectacularly successful war service, Tito defied Stalin; as a reprisal Yugoslavia was expelled from the Cominform in 1948. The leader soon won further international fame as a founder of the non-aligned movement. As a world-class celebrity, Tito mingled affably with everybody from Haile Selassie to Gina Lollobrigida.

In a cluttered Skopje shop window: icons for every occasion.

management and self-governing communes. The vexing nationalities question was met by giving each of the six republics almost complete autonomy in its internal affairs. The foreign policy of nonalignment, under Tito's dynamic leadership, catapulted Yugoslavia to an international signi-ficance far beyond its size or wealth. With Tito's death in 1980, a rotating presidency took over the federal government.

In the 1980s Yugoslavia had to cope with more than its share of serious problems, including a burdensome foreign debt, raging inflation, industrial failings and continuing conflicts of interest between the republics. Yugoslavia's friends, critics and creditors were keeping a close watch.

31

HISTORICAL LANDMARKS

Prehistory	40000-5000 B.C.	Cave men live in present-day Yugoslavia—along the coast, on the islands and inland.
Greek civilization	5th–4th centuries B.C.	Greek travellers meet Illyrian and Thracian tribes. Greeks establish trading colonies along the Adriatic.
Roman Illyria	3rd century B.C.–A.D. 4th century	Romans fight Illyrian pirates, found province of Illyricum. Important Roman settlements at Pula, Salona (Split) and Skopje, among others.
	285-305	Diocletian, from Dalmatia, reigns as Roman emperor.
	395	Roman empire divided; Byzantine influence grows in the Balkans.
Dark Ages	6th–7th centuries	Huns, Avars and Goths force Slavs into Illyria, where Slovenes, Serbs and Croats establish their cultures.
Middle Ages	9th century	King Vlastimir founds a Serbian state. Saints Cyril and Methodius devise an alphabet for the Slavs.
	10th century	Croatians form an independent country. Foundation of a Macedonian state. Hungary and Venice vie for control of Dalmatian coast.
	12th century	Stefan Nemanja founds Serbian dynasty; great churches and monasteries built. Bogomil religion wins converts in Bosnia.
	14th century	Serbia's golden age coincides with the rule of Stefan Dušan.
Turkey Rules		Ottoman Turks invade Balkans. At Battle of Kosovo (1389) Christian defenders bow to Turkish might.

		Turks go on to sweep through Europe.
	15th century	Sarajevo grows and prospers under Turkish domination. Montenegro is ruled by a succession of Orthodox bishops.
	16th century	Dubrovnik thrives as independent city-state.
	17th century	Austrians capture Belgrade from the Turks (1688) as the tide begins to turn.
Napoleon to Hitler	1806	Napoleon occupies Dubrovnik, takes territory in Croatia, Istria and beyond.
	1815	Austria moves in.
	1914	World War I begins in Sarajevo.
	1918	Foundation of Kingdom of Serbs, Croats and Slovenes.
	1929	King Alexander proclaims dictatorship. King assassinated in 1934.
	1941–45	Hitler invades Yugoslavia. King Peter II flees. Tito's partisans liberate the country, establish a people's republic. Tito becomes prime minister.
The New Yugoslavia	1946	New constitution, based on a Soviet model, adopted. (Redrafted in 1953. New constitutions adopted in 1963 and 1974.)
	1948	Tito-Stalin schism; Yugoslavia expelled from Cominform.
	1953	Tito becomes president.
	1961	First summit conference of non-aligned nations held in Belgrade.
	1980	On death of Tito, collective presidency takes control.
	1981	Unrest in autonomous province of Kosovo.

WHERE TO GO

Although it's scarcely bigger than Wyoming or Britain, Yugoslavia is not the sort of place you can get to know in a week or two. There are too many sights really worth seeing; and the bumpy, often mountainous roads between them can drastically curtail your cruising speed.

So, where to begin? If you were going to tour France you'd start in Paris, and your natural base for Britain would be London. But few Yugoslavs would recommend that you launch a tour of their country in Belgrade—unless it's for reasons of airline routing. The national capital is interesting enough on political and cultural grounds, and genuinely worth seeing, but frankly not in the front rank of the country's tourist attractions.

The overwhelming majority of tourists go to the Adriatic coast. Mostly they share the motivation of the millions who crowd the Costas of Spain: they're out for the sun, the swimming and the relaxed way of life. Happily, the Yugoslavian shore still offers plenty of unspoiled elbowroom.

Along the Adriatic you can divide your time between lazy vacation pursuits and some first-

Yugoslavia's most celebrated bridge, a Turkish landmark in Mostar.

34

rate sightseeing: historic cities as priceless as Dubrovnik and Split and islands as fetching as Hvar and Rab. And a day-trip inland gives you quaint Cetinje, or mysterious Mostar, or the ravishing beauty of the Plitvice Lakes.

Nature lovers can't get enough of Yugoslavia, from the Alps of the north to the moody wonders of Lake Ohrid on the Albanian border. The whole country is awash with waterfalls, perforated with caves and gorges, alive with birds and animals. The great outdoors here is conducive to skiing, hiking and "naturism", which is to say lolling about in the sun in the altogether.

Yugoslavia's cultural treasures, generously distributed geographically, range from ancient monuments to modern sculpture. You could spend a week in Serbia, Kosovo and Macedonia touring Orthodox monasteries, with their astonishing hoard of medieval frescoes. Or a week in Dalmatia looking over the Romanesque churches and Venetian palaces.

Our "Where to Go" section divides Yugoslavia into six touristic regions, irrespective of the political boundaries of the country's republics and provinces. While this book makes no attempt at encyclopaedic coverage, all the reasonably accessible highlights have been included.

Whatever your itinerary, leave time for the unforeseen: a detour because of road construction or simple navigational error, or—to be optimistic—an unscheduled delight.

Package tours, usually by comfortable coach, take in most of the leading attractions, eliminating such problems as hotel reservations and language barriers. If you prefer to go it alone, a car obviously provides the greatest flexibility. You can drive your own or choose from international or local hire firms. Buses are inexpensive and allow you to cover much of the same ground, if your plans coincide with their schedules. Less convenient is the Yugoslavian train network, generally not so inviting except for the rugged scenery on the Belgrade–Bar route. The country is big enough to make domestic air travel feasible, for instance on the long hauls between Zagreb and Dubrovnik, or between Belgrade and Skopje, and fares are reasonable. Inside the towns public transport is highly developed and cheap.

Deciding where to stay often hinges on budgetary constraints. If money is no object you can choose to be pampered in international-class luxury hotels, available in the big cities and resorts. At the opposite end of the economy, rooms in private houses are plentiful, potentially cheap and comfortable, and they give you an inside look at local society. Except for the main resorts in July and August, finding a place to stay should pose no special problem. Of course, it's always reassuring to make reservations in advance, but if you arrive roomless at the last moment, the local tourist office should be able to find you accommodation. There's hardly a town without a municipal tourist office and a travel agency or two. Housing problems aside, it's a good idea to check with these experts on the latest local developments, such as museum opening hours and road conditions.

The Essentials

How much of Yugoslavia can you see? A lot depends on how much time you can invest. If you have a week, you might want to spend half of it unwinding by the sea and the rest in the mountains. Or, going from Dubrovnik to Sarajevo, you could compare the architectural legacy of two medieval superpowers, Venice and Turkey. Or, moving from Ljubljana to Zagreb to Belgrade, you could experience the very different cultures of three republics.

Here are a few itineraries to consider; they can be combined at convenient junctions, or shuffled in any number of ways. Inevitably there's an arbitrary and subjective element in our suggestions, but they should start you planning for yourself.

Northern Adriatic
Piran, medieval town
Poreč, Byzantine basilica
Rovinj, old town
Pula, Roman arena
Brioni Islands
(3–5 days)

Dalmatian Coast
Split, Diocletian's Palace
Dubrovnik, walled city
Korčula or Hvar island
(5-7 days)

Montenegro
Bay of Kotor
Budva, walled town
Sveti Stefan resort
Cetinje nostalgia
Lake Skadar
Tara Gorge grandeur
(6–7 days)

The North
Ljubljana culture
Ptuj, old town
Bled Lake and isle
Postojna or Škocjan Caves
Lipica horse stud
(3–5 days)

Inland
Sarajevo minarets
Belgrade city sights
Iron Gates Gorge
Plitvice Lakes
(5–7 days)

NORTHERN ADRIATIC

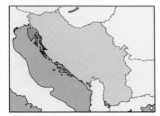

At the top end of Yugoslavia's Adriatic shore bulges the fertile, heart-shaped peninsula of Istria. Geographical realities make this the most heavily touristed part of the country: it's only a hop across the border from Italy or Austria. In haste or at leisure, visitors find here a region rich in all the best Yugoslavia has to offer: beaches, history, culture and colour. And its climate is called the kindest on the whole coast.

Named after a local Bronze Age tribe, the Histri, Istria is part Croatian, part Slovenian and, if intangibly, a bit of Italy, as well. This makes for some linguistic confusion, good food and wine, and encounters with interesting people.

Like so much of Yugoslavia, this region has been fought over for thousands of years. In fact, it's the last chunk of disputed territory to have come under the blue, white and red Yugoslavian

flag, as lately as 1954. Since then the Italian influence has dwindled, but you'll still come across bilingual street signs along with timeless Italianate churches.

If you ever run out of things to see and do on the mainland, convenient ferries go to the northern Adriatic islands, including a couple of perfect gems.

ISTRIA'S WEST COAST*

Starting at the top of the map, **Koper,** the biggest town of Slovenian Istria, successfully leads a double life. It's a fine medieval city with a Venetian stamp, and a modern port and industrial centre.

Motoring into Istria from Trieste or Ljubljana, travellers in a rush may be inclined to bypass Koper, deterred by the puce-coloured high-rise apartment buildings visible across the causeway linking the town with the road south. You can't stop progress, but you can recapture some of the grace of the Middle Ages if you persist into the heart of town.

Founded by the Greeks on an island that was later made into a peninsula, Koper passed through Roman and Slav hands before being taken over by the Venetians in the 13th century. Prosperity

---

* For more information on Istria and its sights, see the Berlitz travel guide to ISTRIA AND CROATIAN COAST.

followed, but a plague in 1551 wiped out two-thirds of the population. After centuries of stagnation, Koper began to revive in 1954, when it became part of Yugoslavia under the London agreement.

From the steamer quay, follow the street called Kidričeva (most of it 16th century), usually crowded with shoppers and tourists. The baroque Palača Belgramoni-Tacco, housing the **Regional Art and Historical Museum** *(Pokrajinski muzej Koper)*, has some paintings by, among others, Vittore Carpaccio, who lived in Koper late in his life, and Gentile Bellini.

As in many other Yugoslavian cities, Koper's main square has been renamed in honour of Marshal Tito. **Titov trg,** at the very centre of the traffic-free historic part of town, gives a brilliant if overblown impression of a classic Venetian piazza. The Venetians ruled Koper (long known as Capodistria) for more than 500 years, so it's understandable that the carved lion of St. Mark is much in evidence.

In the shady arcade of the elegantly pillared **loggia** *(loža)*

Koper's Venetian governor lived in this operatically extravagant palace.

you can sip the local Refoško red wine while admiring, directly across the square, the **Praetorian Palace** *(Pretorova palača)*. Once the residence of the Venetian governor, now the law courts, it started out in the 13th century as two buildings. They were joined 200 years later, but that wasn't the end of it. Local builders added an eruption of artistic afterthoughts, gilding the lily with coats of arms, governors' busts, plaques, and crenellated bristles of no practical or military value.

The imposing but low-rise **cathedral** *(stolnica)*, a century in the construction, wound up Gothic at the bottom and Renaissance above. It is dedicated to an obscure St. Nazarius, whose sarcophagus is found within. Among the art works in the cathedral look for a couple of paintings by Carpaccio. From the top of the massive campanile, which once served as a watch tower, you have an intriguing view of Koper's old streets radiating from the square.

In Koper and nearby Piran you may notice a gross oversupply of butchers' shops. Many of their clients are Italians who cross the border for—of all things—Yugoslavian salami, to slice the weekly food bill. The Yugoslavs, in turn, slip over to Trieste for high-fashion clothing. Traffic at the nearest frontier post, Škofije, is heavy but usually flows smoothly. Its railway and bus station, though outside the town centre, is modern and efficient.

In addition to tourism and trade, Koper prospers from its port (Slovenia's principal outlet to the sea) and industry (car assembly and motorscooter manufacture). Though bathing is possible in Koper itself, most people prefer to cross the bay to Žusterna or better still to Ankaran (20 minutes by motorboat), with its long, sandy beach and excellent campsite.

Going south from Koper, the main road hugs the coastline to **Izola**, 7 kilometres (4 miles) away. Once you get past the titanic industrial smokestack signalling

Finding Your Way	
centar grada	*city centre*
crkva	*church*
kaštel	*castle*
kolodvor	*railway station*
muzej	*museum*
pjaca, placa	*square, plaza*
plaža	*beach*
obala	*quay*
staza	*footpath*
trg	*square*
tržnica	*market*
tvrdjava	*fort*
ulica	*street*
vrato	*gate*
desno	*right*
levo	*left*
pravo	*straight ahead*

a backhanded municipal welcome, the inner old town is pleasant enough. And the port, packed with fishing boats, makes good browsing. Izola's most striking building is the rococo **Palača Besenghi,** an 18th-century wedding-cake confection of stucco and wrought-iron. Not far away is the 16th-century parish church of St. Maurice *(Sveti Mavro),* in which hang paintings by several old masters.

Portorož

The biggest, slickest resort on the Slovenian coast is Portorož, the port of roses. The elegant hotels look even better in this lovely garden setting. Belted by terraced hills covered with vines, olive trees and cypresses, the sheltered bay enjoys a mild climate year-round. Sunbathers unwind on grass, concrete or imported sand, though the brochure image of endless sandy beaches is a slight exaggeration.

This is a dynamic town with a sparkling line-up of activities and entertainment: a casino, many restaurants, cafés and nightspots, a marina for berthing your yacht or hiring one, and thermal baths. Portorož has been known as a health resort since the 13th century, when Benedictine monks used the local salt, mud and brine to treat various ailments. Just breathing the salt air here is said to be therapeutic.

In the town's golden age, around the turn of the 20th century, Portorož found a fashionable niche among European resorts, attracting the cream of Italian and Austrian society. Now rebuilt, it caters to the demands of international "fun" tourism.

For a bit of culture, wander to Seča Point *(Seča Punta),* where outstanding modern sculptures are permanently on view in a park. Artists from many lands have donated their works after participating in the *Forma Viva* sculpture exhibition held here each summer.

Piran

Just 3 kilometres (2 miles) northwest of Portorož but five centuries away in atmosphere, is one of the most appealing historic towns on the Yugoslavian coast. In the back streets, there's nothing contrived to impress the visitor, just haphazard old alleys with twists and turns, and tunnels beneath the upper storeys of connecting houses. A sensitivity to art is revealed by the occasional sculpted window or architectural detail.

A buccaneers' stronghold in the early Middle Ages, Piran's fortifications were gradually extended. Like other towns along this coast, it was under the rule of Venice from the 13th century until the Venetian Republic sank in 1797.

Facing the harbour, the jauntily eccentric **Tartinijev trg** (Tartini Square) is named after the violinist and composer Giuseppe Tartini, who was born here at the end of the 17th century. Alas, poor Tartini! Immortalized by a statue in the middle of the square, the maestro now directs a nonstop traffic jam. The most dazzling building on the square is a 15th-century house painted passionate red, further distinguished by lacy stone carving. High up the wall, an inscription defiantly proclaims: *Lassa pur dir* (Let them talk!). The story goes that a rich Venetian built this house for his mistress, and gossip ensued. It now serves, prosaically, as the tourist office.

The street behind leads up to Piran's largest church, **Sveti Juraj** (St. George's), perched on a bluff with a perfect view over the harbour and the helter-skelter tile roofs of the town. In an effort to keep up with the Venetians, the people of Piran modelled the campanile on the one in Piazza San Marco.

From Tartini Square, walk west along the seafront, past bathers, lively cafés and pastelwashed houses to the Moorishstyle lighthouse. Return through the narrow winding streets of the old quarter. You won't soon run out of sightseeing possibilities in Piran, which has an aquarium and art gallery, a maritime museum and a theatre.

Inland from Piran is **"red Istria"**—the adjective is a nonpolitical reference to the vivid colour of the soil. Even if you're not a farmer or gardener, you'll relish the sight of earth so rich. This region is noted for its white Malvazija and red Teran wines. Here, too, grow some of Europe's most northerly olives, though they're becoming a bit of a rarity; less than one per cent of the millions of fruit trees in Slovenia bear olives.

Novigrad

Down the coast, across the border in Croatia, peaceful Novigrad (New Town) is an *old* town of considerable charm. It's been "new" since the Byzantines took over the Roman town and called it *Neapolis*. When the Croats settled here in the 6th century they merely translated the name, as did the Venetians when they moved in. Only fragments of the town ramparts survived sacking by the Turks in 1687. Underexploited touristically, it's a fishing port with many swimming possibilities. For sightseeing, look in on the basilican church *(Sveti Pelagije)* built on Early Christian foundations. A crypt below the altar holds relics of St. Pelagius, a 3rd-century child martyr.

Harbour of Piran: an Istrian echo of Venice, including the campanile.

Poreč

Thrusting out into the sea on a narrow peninsula, the engaging old town of Poreč is an amazing tourist phenomenon. It has overtaken Opatija and Dubrovnik as Yugoslavia's most popular resort, yet the glorious heart of town is almost untouched. Shrewdly, the authorities have settled the tourists on the periphery, on pine-fringed bays and promontories up and down the coast. Even so, a rash of souvenir shops and throngs of day-trippers are bound to affect the medieval mood of the historic centre. So do the local children, at home with antiquity, bouncing their ball against a 700-year-old Romanesque house.

Poreč's greatest pride, the **Eufrazijeva bazilika** (Basilica of Bishop Euphrasius), is among

the most perfectly preserved of Early Christian churches anywhere. The glittering prize is straight ahead as you enter: gold **mosaics** to rival those of Ravenna or Istanbul. Notice the *Virgin and Child* above the altar and an inlaid image of the Byzantine Bishop Euphrasius himself, holding a somewhat lopsided model of the church he ordered built in the 6th century. (If you detect an unholy glint in his heavy-lidded eye, you may be right: the pope accused him of incest, adultery and murder, not to mention heresy.) Mind where you walk in the basilica; the floor is an obstacle course of what amount to open

Istrian harvest time; double-decker window plants in Izola.

A Gothic bell tower announces the ancient walled town of Motovun.

trap doors revealing earlier mosaics.

Among the church's other treasures: the magnificent ciborium (canopy) with Venetian mosaics, supported by marble columns chosen for their perfectly paired curving stripes. Outside, the atrium is a harmonious oasis of stone in the middle of town. You can climb the adjoining campanile for an angel's-eye view of the whole basilica, including the bishop's palace, the orange-tiled roofs of Poreč, and the coastline.

Strolling along Dekumanska ulica, past ice-cream, souvenir and well-stocked food shops in the ground floors of medieval townhouses, you reach **Marafor trg,** with the scanty remains of

of the Louvre or London's National Portrait Gallery. All propose to capture your likeness for a fee; some are extremely skilled. A guaranteed pretty picture, gratis, is the harbour, crowded with big trawlers, yachts, excursion boats and local water-buses. The harbour is sheltered from winds by the green island of Sveti Nikola (St. Nicholas), a five-minute boat ride away. There you can stay in an 18th-century mansion surrounded by subtropical gardens or your own private bungalow.

All manner of hotels, holiday villages, bungalows and campsites are neatly tucked away along the shores of the Poreč metropolitan tourist zone. The Plava laguna (Blue Lagoon) and Zelena laguna (Green Lagoon) developments, south of Poreč, amass every kind of accommodation and a huge helping of sports facilities—for sailing, speed-boating, skin-diving, horse-riding, tennis, bowling, cycling and even para-skiing. But despite all that's going on, you don't have to move a muscle: just relax in the sun, sampling the local wine.

two Roman temples. The one on the left, thought to be dedicated to the warmongering god Mars, is the largest Roman temple in Istria. The altar from the other, the Temple of Neptune, has been installed in the 18th-century baroque palace that houses the Town Museum *(Gradski muzej)*.

In season, the main sea-front promenade *(Obala Maršala Tita)* attracts street artists painting enough portraits to fill the walls

Sights Inland

The real Istria lies only a short distance inland from the glittering hotels and yacht marinas. Here, the rural way of life—complete with wine, fruit and maize crops, and ploughs drawn

47

by wide-horned white oxen—seems scarcely to have changed for centuries. Many towns and villages have a deserted air nowadays as the young people gravitate to jobs along the coast.

Perhaps the most attractive of the ancient hilltop towns scattered across central Istria is **Motovun**, a 27-kilometre (17-mile) excursion from Poreč. The road corkscrews around a hill up to the towering walls and gate of a castle now earning its keep as a hotel. A 13th-century bell tower looks down on the flagstoned main square, where you'll find an imposing Renaissance church. Take a stroll around the encircling battlements for views of the River Mirna in the valley below, running between oak forests known to gourmets as a rich source of truffles.

An asphalt road leads south to Pazin passing **Beram**, known for its Gothic **frescoes**. Look for the little church of St. Mary of the Rocks *(Sveta Marija na Škriljinah)*, just out of town. The 15th-century compositions *Dance of Death* and *Adoration of the Magi*, attributed to an imaginative painter known as Vincent of Kastav, deserve special attention. They are rich in colour, fantasy and meaningful detail.

A centre of Croatian culture since the Middle Ages, **Pazin** has more of an Austrian than a Venetian feeling. The Germanic counts of Pazin built their castle on the edge of cliffs that plunge straight down to a **chasm** where a whole river vanishes underground. The setting inspired Jules Verne to pitch one of his characters, Mathias Sandorf, over the battlements. He disappeared into the mysterious torrent and later reappeared on the coast—technically impossible, but a nice flight of fanciful fiction.

Stark Sun-Worship

In Yugoslavia, a naturist—known colloquially as a nudist—is given the red-carpet treatment instead of a fig leaf. Official policy regards naturists as a wholesome element in the future of world tourism.

Europe's hotbed of naturism is along the Istrian shore, with Koversada the biggest and best known of undressed resorts. Every August, tanned all over, aspiring beauty queens compete for the title of Miss Koversada, and, for once, the judges wear no more than the contestants.

Enthusiasts from many lands streak to 30 naturist centres along Yugoslavia's coast, from Umag in the north to Ulcinj on the Albanian border, and on several Adriatic islands as well. On maps and direction signs, look for the letters FKK, which identify a beach or camp set aside for naturist buffs.

Vrsar

Back on the coast, Vrsar (barely 9 kilometres or 5½ miles south of Poreč) is more than a village, less than a town. Founded by the Romans, it once served as the summer hideaway of the mighty bishops of Poreč. It became a resort, which the celebrated 18th-century swinger Casanova considered romantic. Now it's a magnet for "naturists". The biggest nudist colony around Vrsar—indeed, it's called the largest in all Europe—is on the isle of **Koversada,** a naked city with everything from restaurants and shops to a post office.

Just south of Vrsar, a narrow inlet called the **Limski kanal** slices

Clad only in hats and sunglasses, naturists work on their tans.

between sheer, pine-topped cliffs for more than 9 spectacular kilometres (6 miles). It's so placid yet stirring that film-makers have turned this location into a simulated Norwegian fjord. These transparent waters are also exploited for farming highly pampered oysters and mussels. The crop may be sampled at "fjordside" restaurants.

Rovinj

The Yugoslav coast can boast some of the most beautiful walled towns in Europe, but photogenic

49

ROVINJ

Rovinj is unwalled; its venerable stone houses clamber right down the slopes of its peninsula to sea level. Of the 15th-century town walls only three gates have survived. At the top of the town, the big baroque church of **St. Euphemia** stands on the site of two earlier churches. Sveta Eufemija contains fragments of a 14th-century marble relief of the patron saint. From its 60-metre (nearly 200-foot-tall) bell tower you can look down on the winding streets, the wide harbour edged by the colourful awnings of the cafés, and 13 little islands scattered near the shore.

A light-hearted town with a large Italian minority, Rovinj has attracted many artists, writers and actors. The port accommodates a merry assortment of hard-working trawlers, ferries, taxi-

boats and pleasure craft. Nearby, the crowded town has solved its traffic problem by reclaiming a spacious rectangle of land from the sea, paving it and calling it a car park.

Belying its carefree atmosphere, Rovinj has been scarred by a troubled history. Its strong defences failed to prevent invasions, in turn, by Dalmatian, Genoese and Uskok pirates.

When it wasn't being pillaged, the town was periodically ravaged by plagues. Having enjoyed relative prosperity as a port under Venetian rule, it was eclipsed by two rivals, Trieste and Pula. The Austrians gave Rovinj a boost in the 19th century by establishing a large tobacco factory and the Marine Biology Institute. Both still operate.

Off the harbour, in the main square, Trg Maršala Tita, the ornate Balbi Arch (1680) was one of three town gates. The baroque town hall now houses the Gradski muzej (Town Museum), with old and modern paintings, a library and period furniture. Pass under the Balbi Arch and wander through the old **Venetian quarter** with its quaint piazzas and steep lanes.

Botanists and nature lovers enjoy the rare Mediterranean flora in a large park south of Rovinj, on the Muntrav promontory. The quarries nearby once supplied stone for the Doges' Palace in Venice.

Most of Rovinj's hotels (one with a casino) occupy the piney shore south of the town and the two largest islands offshore. Katarina, the closest isle, is a popular bathing place. The largest, Crveni Otok (Red Island), is ac-

The catch of the day comes ashore in the quaint port of Rovinj.

tually a pair of isles linked by a causeway. One of the two, uninhabited, is reserved for naturists. The other has a luxury hotel complex, incorporating a former Benedictine monastery.

PULA

It may not be the biggest in the world, but Pula's Roman amphitheatre is an awesome sight, looming larger than you'd ever imagine. Though imperfectly preserved, this perfect oval of a coliseum sets the scene for a city proud of its distinguished history.

Not that Pula lives in the past. Istria's biggest town (population 60,000) is a natural centre of modern tourism. With an international airport 6 kilometres (4 miles) away and holiday facilities burgeoning up and down the coast, Pula is converting Adriatic sunshine into German marks and U.S. dollars. Still, the ancient port's biggest industry remains shipbuilding.

The origins of Pula go back to the age of Greek mythology. In the legend of the Golden Fleece, when Jason and Medea made off with their loot, Medea's father sent several ships in pursuit. It seems one crew abandoned the chase here, preferring to live happily ever after with the local Illyrian maidens. Whether or not these defectors were really the founders of Pula, a settlement

existed here as early as 500 B.C. The first fort was raised on the hill now occupied by the *kaštel,* a 17th-century fortress. From there the settlement spread down to the shore in concentric circles, a pattern still visible on the modern map.

The Roman legions arrived in 178 B.C., incorporating Istria into metropolitan Rome. Under frequently changing rulers, Pula struggled through hard times until the Austrians took over at the end of the 18th century. The city was revitalized as the chief port and naval base of the empire. In this optimistic atmosphere, a young Irish writer keen on Greek mythology came to Pula to teach English at the Berlitz School. But James Joyce wasn't really cut out for pedagogy; his career here lasted but a matter of months.

Start your sightseeing at Pula's most enduring landmark, the great Roman **arena** *(amfiteater).* Its golden shell has dominated the waterfront since the 1st century. According to the ancient rumour mill, Emperor Vespasian rebuilt and enlarged the amphitheatre to please his local mistress, a Pula girl called Antonia Cenida. About 23,000 fans could be seated for gladiator fights and contests between wild beasts and Christians. Today there are seats enough for a rock concert, or the Yugoslavian Film Festival. Lacking only a convertible roof, this classic amphitheatre has just about everything a modern audience could want.

In the basement (actually at present-day street level) a maze of passages leads to the chambers where the "performers" awaited their cue. Now there are exhibits of Roman artefacts unearthed hereabouts, including wine presses and enough amphoras to have given the whole town a hangover.

The main street running past the arena leads to the enthusiastically named Brotherhood and Unity Square *(Trg Bratstva-jedinstva)*. Experts familiar with the works of Dante might recognize this as the site of the necropolis mentioned in the *Inferno* (9th canto). Now the centre of modern Pula, it's flanked by massive city fortifications. The double arch nearby serves as the entrance to the **Archaeological Museum** *(Arheološki muzej)*, showing sophisticated Roman sculpture and mosaics as well as prehistoric relics. These include idols and spearheads left by cavemen who settled near the site of Pula airport about 40,000 years before the first flight landed there. On the hillside behind the museum are the remains of a 2nd-century Roman theatre.

At the beginning of Prvomajska ulica (May Day Street) stands a **triumphal arch** erected in the 1st century B.C. to honour three soldier brothers of the Sergi family. A tenacious breed, this clan seems to have dominated Pula for more than a thousand years. If you take a picture of the elaborately carved monument with its two pairs of Corinthian columns, you're joining an old tradition; it has been studied and sketched by Michelangelo, Piranesi and the 18th-century Scottish architect Robert Adam.

St. Mary's Chapel *(Sveta Marija Formosa)* is all that remains of a 6th-century basilica built by a local son (Maximian) who was to become archbishop of Ravenna and eventually a saint. Many of the church's treasures were carried off to Venice, including the four alabaster columns that now grace the high altar of St. Mark's. The chapel contains 6th-century mosaics and 15th-century frescoes.

Further along Prvomajska, up a steep side street on the right, stands **Sveti Franjo,** a Franciscan monastery church of the early 14th century. Its splendid west portal is decorated with carved shells. Hanging over the street, a twin pulpit catered for overflow congregations in the days before public address systems. The 15th-century wooden altarpiece is called the finest Venetian Gothic sculpture in Istria.

The first thing you'll see in Trg Republike (Republic Square), which used to be the Roman

Forum, is the perfectly preserved **Temple of Augustus** *(Augustov hram)*, with its slender Corinthian columns. This cool, dignified treasure has survived 19 centuries, but the Temple of Diana that stood next to it is now only a shadowy outline on the back of the Gothic town hall. Nearby, the **cathedral** retains the austere simplicity of the 6th-century basilica from which it evolved.

Crowning the hill in the centre of the city is the **kaštel**. It occupies the site of the original Illyrian settlement, which became in turn the location of the Roman capitol. In the 13th century the ambitious Sergi family pulled down the Roman buildings to make room for their own castle. In retribution, many of the Sergi were massacred one night in 1271 by a rival political faction; the rest were expelled some 60 years later when Venice took over the city.

The present star-shaped castle, designed for the Venetians by a French engineer in the 17th century, is now assigned to the Museum of the National Revolution *(Muzej narodne revolucije)*. You can rest under the trees here and contemplate Pula's magnificent harbour.

Pedestrians ignore a Roman triumphal arch in the centre of Pula.

The town beaches, mostly pebble, are at nearby Stoja and Zelenika. Most tourists choose to stay just outside the city at one of the well-planned holiday villages, each with its own character. The largest and closest of them is Zlatne Stijene, a complex of hotels and bungalows with extensive entertainment and sports facilities.

Brioni Islands

From the old fishing village of Fažana (8 kilometres or 5 miles north of Pula) it's only 15 minutes by boat to the peaceful, historic Brioni *(Brijuni)* archipelago. The 14 islands now comprise a national park, open to foreign tourists since 1984. Before that, only VIPs visited the place; Marshal Tito made Brioni his retreat for 30 years.

Tito's mahogany-panelled 45-metre yacht is berthed in the harbour of **Veliki Brijun,** the biggest island. A photo gallery in the local museum documents Tito's life here, at work, relaxing, and entertaining heads of state and celebrities like Queen Elizabeth II, Nikita Khrushchev, Fidel Castro and Sophia Loren.

Deer wander down to the pier to gape as every boatload of tourists arrives. Among other animals in the island's population are lions, giraffe and zebra, visible on a tour of the **safari park** and **zoo.** Veliki Brijun is noted for its mouflon (big-horned sheep), fallow deer and pheasants. On a warm day they welcome the shade of the forests of Aleppo pine, cedar, eucalyptus and stately old holm oak trees. But the main arboreal attraction is an olive tree said to be 1,600 years old. Long before it was planted, aristocratic Romans were enjoying their summer villas here; you can roam around the spacious **ruins.**

The island's mission as a tourist destination, so recently revived, goes back to 1893 when Veliki Brijun was bought by a Viennese steel magnate. He spent a fortune taming the scenery, installing utilities and building hotels. When a malaria epidemic seemed to doom the project, Dr. Robert Koch, the medical pioneer who discovered the cause of tuberculosis, was invited over to eradicate the disease. (A memorial bas-relief here honours the doctor.) With health restored, Veliki Brijun was soon all but overrun by Europe's nobles and notables, enjoying the discreet luxury of a trendy new resort.

When World War II broke out the Italian and German navies took over from the fleeing tourists. Because the islands acquired a concentration of Axis military forces, including a fleet of about a hundred assault boats, the Allies bombed them three times. It took years to repair all the damage.

ISTRIA'S EAST COAST

From Pula the 103-kilometre (64-mile) road to the port of Rijeka winds inland through wild and changing Mediterranean scenery, from mountainsides fragrant with pines to beaches lapped by the sea. Once you've looked down on the islands of the gulf, though, there's nothing much of touristic importance until you reach the Kvarner Riviera, renowned for its mild climate.

Mošćenička Draga, the first of a string of resorts at the foot of Mount Učka, is an authentic old fishing village successfully converted to tourist town. The nets still dry along the quay on which the holiday-makers promenade.

Another little resort, **Medveja,** has a pebble beach that is perhaps the finest on this coast. **Lovran,** so named for its surrounding laurel groves, neatly combines seaside pursuits and a dash of history. Just a short stroll up from the waterfront, you go through the original **town gate** into the core of the old town. Its buildings slightly askew, Lovran exudes a haphazard medieval charm. In the parish church of St. George (Sveti Juraj) there are admirable Gothic wall paintings.

Opatija

A resort in the grand manner, Opatija trails clouds of 19th-century glory. As a favourite winter retreat of central Europe-

No shortage of peace and quiet along 2,000 kilometres of Adriatic shore.

an high society, it acquired smart hotels and opulent villas in every fanciful style. Emperor Franz Joseph, no less, used to visit his mistress here. But came the tourist revolution! The winter palaces that used to ensconce aristocrats are now the summer watering places of ordinary citizens, mostly Germans.

New hotels built since the war have scarcely altered the town's gracious Edwardian appearance.

Most of the swimming is from an expanded and improved concrete lido; inviting enough, but Opatija is not the ideal place for bathers who require a real beach.

Opatija (meaning "abbey") started as a fishing village alongside the medieval abbey of St. James, of which a tiny, much-

57

restored church remains. In 1844 a Rijeka businessman built the neo-classical Villa Angiolina nearby; news about this idyllic corner spread, and soon Opatija could hardly cope with all the visiting tycoons and duchesses. The businessman's estate, now called Park Prvi Maj (First of May Park), is the place to foil the summer heat in the shade of giant sequoia and Himalayan cypress trees.

Since the end of the 19th century Opatija has been known as a year-round health resort, thanks to the high mineral content of the sea and the iodine in the fresh air. The annual average of 2,230 hours of sunshine may have something to do with it. Before World War I the town had 12 sanatoriums. Since 1959 the tradition has been continued by an organization called Thalassotherapia, which can treat what ails you, whether it's a cardiac, pulmonary or rheumatic problem.

Apart from therapeutic pursuits Opatija caters for a wide range of tastes, from opera (performances in the open-air theatre by the sea) to motorcycle racing (at nearby Preluk). As a change from swimming, sailing and water-skiing, you can climb or drive up Mount Učka, the source of refreshing summer breezes and a barrier against cold winter winds.

RIJEKA

After the escapism of all those charming, leisurely little ports along Istria's holiday coast, Rijeka comes as something of a shock. With a population above 200,000, Yugoslavia's largest port is all muscle: enormous cranes, a dry dock, cavernous international car-ferries and workaday trawlers. Facing all this is a panorama of Italianate buildings as pompous as an operetta admiral in full regalia.

For a city of this size and antiquity—it was the site of the Roman town of *Tarsatica*—Rijeka has few ancient monuments. Blame an earthquake, two world wars and an assortment of miscellaneous misfortunes. But there's enough left to merit a couple of hours of sightseeing... especially if you're between ships, planes or trains.

To simplify Rijeka's recent, complicated history: in the 15th century, it developed as a prosperous Austrian port under the Habsburgs, rivalling Trieste and Venice. Three centuries later it passed under Hungarian control, a status that endured until World War I, interrupted by brief periods of Croatian and French rule. Rijeka is known in Italian as Fiume (both names mean "riv-

A sunny sanctuary in Yugoslavia's biggest, busiest port, Rijeka.

er"). In the 1920s the border between Italy and Yugoslavia was drawn right through the town, along the River Rječina and its tributary known as the Mrtvi kanal (Dead Channel). Finally, after World War II the badly bombed city was reunited under Yugoslavian rule.

Parallel to the steamer quay, the main shopping street, the **Korzo,** invites leisurely strolling. The biggest crowds come out at day's end for the great Mediterranean walkabout. Look for a clock tower known locally as Pod uriloj (under the clock), atop a medieval gate. This leads to the old town, a hodgepodge of decaying tenements, bombed-out open spaces, a very few historical relics and incongruous modern commercial buildings. Among the remaining highlights is a 13th-century cathedral, much remodelled in later times, with a free-standing bell tower. What distinguishes the tower is the way it lists from the vertical—though the tilt is no competition for Pisa.

The circular baroque church of St. Vitus *(Sveti Vid)*, nearby, contains a famous wooden statue of the Crucifixion from an earlier church. The story goes back seven centuries. In 1296, a local gambler named Petar Lančarić, furious at a bad run of cards, launched a stone at the figure on the cross, which was seen to bleed. The ground outside the church immediately swallowed the blasphemer, so the legend goes, except for his pitching hand, which was cut off and burned. A stone can be seen adhering to the statue's side.

At the top of the town, **Trsat gradina** marks the site of the original Illyrian settlement. It's easier to reach the castle by car or bus than by foot; you have to climb 536 steps. Early in the 19th century an Austrian vice-marshal of Anglo-Irish ancestry, Laval Nugent, bought the medieval castle and adapted it to his bizarre tastes. The little classical temple he built inside, using Doric columns from Pula, was intended as his mausoleum. Today it serves as a bandstand, and the whole place is now a restaurant. So it goes.

On a rise near the castle stands the 15th-century church of **St. Mary** *(Sveta Marija Lauretanska)*, which has long been a popular shrine with high-climbing pilgrims. According to legend the Virgin Mary's house rested here for three years in the 13th century, on its miraculous journey from Nazareth to Loreto, Italy. The painting of the Madonna adorning the high altar was presented to the town by the urbane Pope Urban V. The Franciscan monastery next door contains hundreds of curious votive offerings to St. Mary, mainly from grateful sailors. Rijeka has always been a seafaring town.

NORTHERLY ISLANDS

Yugoslavia claims more than a thousand Adriatic islands, rocks and reefs. At last count, 66 of them were inhabited. The sparkling Kvarner Gulf, separating Istria from the Croatian mainland, has four main islands, each provided with pleasant beaches and colourful old towns.

Though geographers take the liberty of lumping them together, each isle can claim a character and history of its own. The gulf is where you'll find Yugoslavia's largest island—bigger than Malta or the Isle of Wight. It goes under a most improbable name:

Krk

The terse title, pronounced something like the Scottish "kirk", belongs to an island big and hilly enough to thrust bald highlands above the treeline. Of course, that's not snow up top, just white rock. And although the northeastern shore, whipped by an unkind wind, is bare limestone, other parts of the island look green and inviting.

Krk is linked to the mainland by a daring double-arched bridge that soars twice, catching its breath on a barren island halfway across the sea. The toll bridge (named after Tito) makes Krk's airport handy for Rijeka and nearby resorts. It also brings closer the mainland's industrial coast, just south of Rijeka. Luckily, the towering smokestacks and flaming oil refinery are invisible from the tourist areas.

With water supplied by two small lakes and a river, Krk is one Adriatic island that can drink heartily. Thirst may have been on the minds of the Stone Age travellers who settled in caves near Baška and Vrbnik. The island's heyday came in the early Middle Ages when the lords of Krk, the ambitious Frankopan family, bulldozed their way to control along the mainland coast as well. In 1480 one of the Frankopans, consolidating his many-castled assets, ceded Krk to the Venetians. The island thereafter coasted along as a freshwater backwater. But Krk's influence on Croatian culture has always been strong. Some of the oldest tomes in the ancient Glagolitic alphabet, the first form of writing used by the Slavs, were inscribed here.

Following the practice of many of the islands, **Krk** is the name of the town, too. In Roman times it was officially recognized as a full-fledged municipality; a stone engraving refers to the *Splendidissima Civitas Curictarum* (Splendid City of the Krkers). Inside the walls of the jumbled old town (the twisting, hilly lanes are very un-Venetian) you'll find the long, low Bishop's Palace and the 12th-century Frankopan castle.

The present **cathedral** was built in the same era, atop Roman baths. It is noted for a Gothic silver screen showing the Madonna in glory and the beautifully carved capitals of its Roman pillars. Through a trap door in a side chapel you can see a mosaic floor from the baths. A narrow, arched passageway links the cathedral to the curious, two-storey basilica of **St. Quirinus** *(Sveti Kvirin)*. The simple 10th-century lower level, long a wine cellar, was restored in 1963. The Romanesque upper church, built a century later, spans the passageway. You enter through the bell tower, topped by an incongruous onion dome on which perches an outsize trumpeting angel. The square tower across the street is 12th century, which makes it the oldest part of the *kaštel*. From the 16th-century round tower you have views of the sea and city. The rest of the castle is a roofless shell laid out as the bishop's garden, next to his palace.

Elsewhere on the island, Punat, guarding the entrance to a sheltered bay, has become a lively tourist centre in its own right. Vrbnik, the only sizable east-coast settlement, has defied all comers from its clifftop for 800 years. But Krk's fastest-growing resort area is on the north-west coast, which claims the glamorous **Haludovo** hotel-village.

The northernmost settlement on Krk, Omišalj, was one of the Frankopan hilltop strongholds.

Its medieval quarter, little changed over the centuries, centres on the main square and Romanesque church of St. Mary.

Cres and Lošinj

Once connected by a narrow strip of land, later separated by a canal and now reunited by a bridge, Cres and Lošinj are anything but the Siamese twins you might imagine. Cres, the second largest of the Adriatic islands in area but underpopulated, is mostly arid limestone hills. Tiny Lošinj, on the other hand, has luxuriant vegetation and more than twice as many inhabitants.

Even by Yugoslavian standards the 83-kilometre (52-mile) drive from the car ferry at Porozina in northern Cres to the town of Veli Lošinj down south is hairraising. In one area the road teeters along the top of a ridge with a sheer drop to the sea on either side. The passengers, if not the driver, can enjoy some memorable vistas. This road, linking almost all the settlements previously dependent on boat services, has given a big boost to tourism.

The town of **Cres**, an old fishing port, was Crespa to the Romans and Cherso to the Venetians, who ruled here for centuries. The main town gate, beneath a venerable clock tower, leads to the closely packed streets typical of medieval walled cities. Straight ahead, hemmed in by old houses,

Backwoods holiday: campers escape life's pressures in Mali Lošinj.

stand the campanile and church of St. Mary of the Snows *(Majka Božja Sniježne)*, built in the 15th century. The tiny church of Sveti Sidar, in the maze of streets on the right, has a remarkable wooden statue of St. Isidore (to whom the church is dedicated).

Osor, a tiny village on the straits separating Cres and Lošinj, was once a Roman city of 20,000 and the seat of a bishop. But the Venetian rulers moved their capital north to Cres; finally, Osor's doom was assured by the ravages of pirates and malaria. The early Renaissance cathedral and the remains of extensive city walls indicate the dimensions of Osor's past glory. This is a happy digging ground for archaeologists. Some of the

Rab's fetching skyline: campaniles, red-tiled roofs and treetops.

artefacts on view in the local museum were unearthed by Sir Richard Burton, a Victorian explorer and celebrity.

Over the bridge and you're in Lošinj. The center of gravity for tourists leans to the south, around **Mali Lošinj** and **Veli Lošinj** (the names translate as Little and Big Lošinj, though in modern times the population tables are turned). Aside from the expectable dash of history, they have some inviting tourist facilities and beaches.

The mild, sunny winters began to attract holiday-makers and asthma sufferers more than a century ago. At the time, Austria ruled, and Mali Lošinj had six large shipyards and a fleet of 150 ships. The indented shoreline and

Rab

This curtly-named island offers history and scenery. Though the highlands and some of the coastal extremities are bleached bleak and desolate, most of Rab's interior is a summary of classic Mediterranean landscape—complete with vineyards, fig and olive trees and refreshing pine woods. And perhaps best of all, the principal town (called Rab, of course) transports you to a more gracious and leisurely age.

Settled successively by the Illyrians, Greeks and Romans, the island spent the Middle Ages alternating between the rule of Venice and the kingdom of Croatia. Venice finally won. In 1920, after more than a century under Austrian control, Rab became part of Yugoslavia.

With its four campaniles rising above the narrow promontory, the town of **Rab** might be a graceful four-masted schooner sailing out to sea. Real sailboats—and professional fishing boats—give the peaceful waterfront a hint of adventure. Since there are no cars in the old town, the atmosphere is perfect for wandering and reflecting. At first you may think it's a warren of stone, but in the thick of medieval Rab there are even spaces for gardens; see the roses tumbling over the tops of walls. Take time to appreciate the details—the design of the windows, the door-

transparent sea give Mali Lošinj a modern role as a centre for scuba diving.

A short boat trip from here will take you to the curious island of Susak, which appears to be little more than a sandbank. Geologists are still arguing about how it evolved. Although it may sound barren, the isle is covered with terraced vineyards. Susak is famous for its wine and bright, mini-skirted folk costumes.

65

ways, the sculptural decorations on the houses. As for the larger picture, the glowing cream-coloured stone, deep blue sky and brilliant oleanders are as harmonious as the setting.

The three principal streets run parallel, one above the other; the middle one is the main shopping street. The highest, along the ridge of the promontory, has no less than six churches. The pink-and-white striped façade near the end of the street belongs to the former cathedral, **St. Mary Major** *(Sveta Marija Velika)*. An outstanding example of a small Romanesque basilica, it was consecrated by Pope Alexander III, in person, in 1177. Note the expressive Gothic *Pietà* over the doorway, the 15th-century choir stalls and a six-sided canopy with 9th-century stone carving. The cathedral is the setting for recitals during the summer-long festival, Rab Musical Evenings; the acoustics are grand, except when a disco down the hill unleashes its decibels in competition. Near the cathedral, the tallest and most beautiful of four bell towers dates from the 12th century. On each of its four "floors" the arched Romanesque windows are different.

An 11th-century convent, still housing Benedictine nuns (you can hear but not see them at prayer) faces Trg Slobode (Freedom Square). This is the dividing line between old Rab and New Town *(Novi grad)*, some of which is as new as the 14th century. The area of lanes and passageways known as Kaldanac, the most ancient part of Rab, was walled off in the 15th century to keep the plague from spreading. The place has been half-deserted ever since, as the bricked-up windows and doorways confirm.

Rajska plaža (Paradise Beach), the finest beach on the island, sprawls beside the San Marino hotel complex. This is named after a 4th-century citizen of Rab who, tradition says, founded San Marino, the world's smallest republic.

The road from Rab town north-west to Kampor goes past the old monastery of St. Euphemia and the impressive Cemetery of the Victims of Fascism *(Groblje Žrtava Fašizma)*. The Italians established a concentration camp on this spot in 1942. Pine and cypress trees shade the long, crowded rows of gravestones of 4,500 victims. A powerful mosaic by the Slovenian artist Marij Pregelj (1913-67) expresses the agony of it all.

A popular boat trip from Rab goes to the island of **Pag,** noted for its sharply flavoured ewe's milk cheese *(Paški sir)*. In ancient times Pag supported large Roman communities, and it was prosperous enough to be fought over in the Middle Ages. Today, though, much of Pag looks like a vision from the Arctic instead of the Adriatic—cruel white rock with scarcely enough overgrowth to shade a lizard. But there are oases, and sizable flocks of sheep graze among any clumps of grass they find.

Another industry peculiar to the island is delicate lacework. Pag lace used to be shipped directly to the imperial court at Vienna. The local women still wear their traditional costumes, with lace caps... and not just to impress the tourists. The insularity of the people of Pag persists, in spite of the construction of a modern bridge joining the island to the mainland.

Shawls, tablecloths, antimaccassars, all hand made on the island of Krk.

DALMATIA

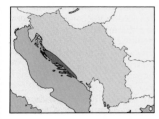

Sunny Dalmatia has all the luck: more coastline, more scenery and more majestic monuments than any other part of Yugoslavia. The people of the province—tough but hospitable fishermen and farmers—haven't quite become accustomed to the consequent tourist boom.

The coast twists into countless coves and inlets hiding fishing villages, medieval walled towns and beaches. Behind the narrow coastal strip looms a barrier of rugged mountains, pierced by spectacular canyons with thundering waterfalls. Offshore, Dalmatia's Adriatic is strewn with green-terraced islands as beautiful as they are historic.

With minor gerrymandered exceptions, virtually all of Dalmatia comes within the domain of the republic of Croatia. But nearly everybody has had a go at ruling this strip of coast, starting with the Illyrians, Greeks, Romans and Slavs. In recent centuries Venetians and Austrians took turns dominating Dalmatia.

We survey the best of the province's sights, from north-west to south-east along the coast, starting with a distinguished town where medieval and modern buildings crowd together almost compatibly.

ZADAR

Fate has mellowed Zadar, an important port that's been coveted, conquered and reconstructed time and again. Between the 8th and 16th centuries, typically, it changed hands 30 times. The most recent run of bad luck explains the juxtaposition of old and new architecture: in World War II Zadar was bombed on 72 occasions. After the dust settled, they filled in most of the gaps with inoffensive modern buildings and parks.

Ancient Zadar, once the capital of Dalmatia, is bounded on three sides by the sea. Grey defensive walls still line the narrow harbour, almost closed off by a breakwater. While the port side, facing the modern town, bustles with the traffic of cars, ferries and pleasure boats, the seaward shore is a relaxed, leafy promenade.

Roman colonists who arrived in the 1st century B.C. laid out a rigid grid of streets surrounding a magnificent **forum**, nearly as big as a playing field. From the ruins that remain rise the stumps of

69

three Corinthian columns and a fourth pillar, intact; until the late 19th century it served as the municipal pillory, to which offenders were chained for punishment and ridicule. But look more closely: you'll see the foundations of what were artisans' shops along the edges of the square, and a wealth of stone relics spread about, including empty sarcophagi and finely carved fragments from collapsed walls and columns.

Stonework from the forum was recycled in the columns supporting the massive, circular church dedicated to **St. Donatus** *(Sveti Donat)*, a local bishop. (It's not

Art and faith converge in Zadar's silver sarcophagus of St. Simeon.

every old church where you can discern pagan inscriptions to Jupiter and Juno.) This imposing structure, begun in the early 9th century, is empty now except for archaeological exhibits. Summer concerts sometimes take place here. Roam around St. Donatus, inside and out, and judge the eccentric geometry of the plan—three semi-circular apses bulging from a rotunda.

An even bigger church near the forum features a splendid Romanesque façade with rows of blind arcades and two rose windows. The cathedral of **St. Anastasia** *(Sveta Stošija)* was built in the 12th and 13th centuries on the site of an earlier church. Inside it's dark and relatively austere except for some stone-carving; look for the 9th-century sarcophagus of St. Anastasia herself in the left apse. Notable here are the Gothic choir stalls before the main altar and the 14th-century canopy above it.

Zadar's Archaeological Museum *(Arheološki muzej),* founded in the early 19th century, has acquired a big collection of Roman and early Croatian antiquities. Next to it is **St. Mary's Basilica** *(Sveta Marija)*, which belongs to a chapter of Benedictine nuns established by a Croatian noblewoman in the 11th century. Priceless liturgical vessels known as the Silver and Gold of Zadar are kept here.

And one last church for tireless sightseers: **Sveti Frane,** reconstructed several times. Although it's nothing to rave about architecturally, the 13th-century Franciscan monastery church does possess some valuable paintings and, in its treasury, a worthy collection of illuminated psalters, early printed books and eucharistic vessels. St. Francis himself is supposed to have visited Zadar in 1219.

Only a few years earlier the knights of the Fourth Crusade had sacked the town. The wily Venetian doge masterminded the pillage. He recruited the crusaders by giving them the ships to take them to the Holy Land. Later, Venice bought rights in Dalmatia for 100,000 ducats. Venetian military engineers promptly turned Zadar into a formidable stronghold: a massive fortress straddled the neck of land linking the town and mainland. Existing moats were converted into reservoirs, and new ones were excavated—a system of defence the Turks found impregnable. After Venice, the Austrians took over, followed by the Italians. Zadar didn't become part of Yugoslavia until after World War II.

An important feature of life in Zadar, as elsewhere in Yugoslavia, is the **marketplace,** where kerchiefed peasant women weigh out cherries, peaches, beans, tomatoes, or whatever happens to

be in season. Business goes on here from dawn until midday, when the farmers pack up their baskets and go home. Even if you're not in the market for groceries, the market is worth a stop.

As a holiday destination Zadar has bounded ahead in recent years. In the pattern of other resorts along this coast, most of the hotels are located outside the urban area. The biggest concen-

tration of tourist establishments occupies the wooded promontory of Borik, with a sandy beach and lively activities.

Thirty kilometres (18 miles) down the coast from Zadar, the small resort of **Biograd-na-Moru** (White City by the Sea) has plenty of experience at entertaining visitors. Its popular beach twists into a sandy cove, edged by dense pine woods. There's little to show that ten centuries back Biograd

In the hinterland of northern Dalmatia, near Benkovac, a cattle fair attracts a crowd.

was a royal town, residence of the medieval Croatian kings. When Croatia and Hungary were united under a single crown in 1102, King Koloman travelled to Biograd for his coronation. But shortly after, in a demonstration of power, the Venetian doge had the town levelled to its foundations. Destroyed a second time by the Turks in the 17th century, Biograd never recovered its former glory.

ŠIBENIK

Arriving by sea at the historic town of Šibenik, you can appreciate the nautical and aesthetical perfection of the setting. Ranks of islands form the outer defences, and then the ship slips

73

past steep grey cliffs into a wide lagoon. The red-tiled roofs of the town ascend the wooded slopes to a complex of forts. But it takes more than an impregnable position to save a town from disaster: siege, fire, plague and bombardment have all taken their toll in the course of Šibenik's thousand-year history.

The town is first mentioned in connection with a Croatian assembly held here in the generally fateful year of 1066. In the next century, the Croatian-Hungarian kings gave Šibenik a charter granting local privileges. Even after the Venetians had taken over, the townsfolk managed to hold on to some of those rights.

In the 16th century the plague did its worst: barely one-sixth of the population of 10,000 survived. The Turks tried to take the town a number of times, but their assaults were repulsed from the formidable hill fortresses. In 1797 the Austrians moved in, and stayed until the end of World War I. World War II meant four more years of occupation and heavy bombing. Since then, Šibenik's fortunes have clearly changed: its vigorous industrial growth and burgeoning tourist trade have completely transformed the region.

Fortunately, the old part of town has changed little in the past thousand years. Centuries of calamity convinced the people to use durable building materials, resistant to fire, water and cannon balls. Sturdy houses of stone rise in tiers, and staircases scale the steep hill from the waterfront to the Fort of St. Anne on the craggy summit.

But first, see Šibenik's most glorious monument. **St. James's Cathedral** *(Sveti Jakov)* was begun in the 15th century. The accomplished architect and sculptor Juraj Dalmatinac (George the Dalmatian) can take credit for the cathedral's best features, including a most intriguing sculptural innovation. A narrow **frieze** going around the outer walls of the apses features 74 heads of stone: a rogues' gallery, it's said, of townsfolk who neglected to donate to the building fund. These are candid portraits. Some of the citizens look frightened, as if startled by a flashbulb, others seem angry, but a few are able to summon a smile.

Flanking the cathedral's side portal, carved lions hold up pedestals supporting the Romanesque figures of Adam and Eve, rescued from an earlier cathedral on the site. Inside, slender Gothic columns separate the aisles from the spacious nave, which is

Fig leaves at the ready, Adam and Eve stand guard at Šibenik cathedral.

bathed in iridescent light from the stained-glass window overhead. The unique barrel-vaulted roof is constructed solely of huge slabs of stone, which run the length of the structure. The **baptistery,** a tiny chamber of ribbed conches, converging crescents and Gothic tracery, is another work of Dalmatinac, a native of Zadar who designed palaces and chapels on both shores of the Adriatic. He is honoured here by a statue in front of the church, the work of Ivan Meštrović, Yugoslavia's greatest sculptor.

In the square, café clients enjoy the shade of the arcaded loggia, which is often used as a backdrop for summer performances. Of interest to archaeology buffs, the **Town Museum** *(Gradski muzej)*, former residence of the Venetian administrator, shows off a collection of neolithic artefacts unearthed in the vicinity. Other exhibits are devoted to the work of Juraj Dalmatinac, the master of stonework and town planning.

An easy side-trip from Šibenik goes up the Krka River (by boat, bus or car) to the refreshing **Krka Falls** *(Slapovi Krke)*. Don't expect Niagara. But the falls are impressive in their own way. In addition to a series of roaring cataracts there are cascades tame enough to swim in or shower under, an appealing idea on a hot day. Framing the spectacle are peaceful lakes and rich green forests. At the most visited spot souvenir vendors operate an informal bazaar next to a restaurant-with-a-view.

TROGIR

The ancient town of Trogir may remind you of an island paradise. In spite of a couple of discrepancies—a bridge connects it to the mainland, and the palm trees along the seafront promenade are not indigenous—the impression persists. Trogir is a different sort of paradise, for collectors of art, history and charm.

In the 3rd century B.C. Greek settlers named this place *Tragurion,* a reference to the goats grazing here. One vestige of Trogir's founders is a bas-relief, now in the Benedictine convent, of the Greek god of opportunity. A very slippery fellow, he shaved the back of his head so that once he got past you there was little chance of catching him again.

The Roman empire replaced Greek domination. Then came Byzantines, Croats, Croato-Hungarians, and, in 1420, the Venetians who stayed for nearly four centuries. The Austrians ruled

Swimmers venture into one of the cool, refreshing backwaters of the Krka Falls complex.

from 1797 to 1918, except for a brief French interlude. During the early Venetian era Trogir's best buildings went up in a flurry of conspicuous creativity.

This compact gallery of medieval architecture draws you immediately into a web of narrow streets and vaulted passageways; the airspace between buildings doesn't go to waste here. Of all Trogir's beautifully preserved cultural monuments—churches, palaces and official buildings—the imperative one is the cathedral of **St. Lawrence** *(Sveti Lovrijenac)*, built between the 13th and 15th centuries. Don't miss the Romanesque **main portal,** a self-contained work of genius. On either side of the doorway stand Adam and Eve wearing fig leaves and very worried faces, with thick-maned lions at their feet. A local sculptor named Radovan was responsible for this creative climax, dated 1240. The campanile was built and rebuilt in various stages over several centuries; just when it was looking good Venetian cannonballs lopped off the top.

Inside the cathedral, a ciborium forms a striking two-storey canopy over the main altar. The pulpit, elevated on eight slender columns, dates back to the 13th century. A Trogir wood-carver fashioned the choir stalls in the 15th century. For a Renaissance highlight, pause at the chapel of St. John Orsini, where robust stone cherubs playfully thrust torches through half-open doors.

On Trogir's main square, the column-fronted **loggia** also dates from the 15th century. It served as courthouse—the judge's bench and table are still in place—and provided a stage for the town crier. On the western side of the square the **Palača Ćipiko** presents a fine façade—two sets of triple Gothic windows, one above the other. Inside the palace you'll find a wooden rooster, a figurehead from the prow of a Turkish ship captured in battle.

Tiny Trogir is made for meandering; you can see it all in a couple of hours. Fishermen mend their nets along the quay, which ends abruptly at the sturdy **Kamerlengo Fortress** *(Kula Kamerlengo)*, built in the 15th century to head off pirates and Turks. Now the mood is incomparably more relaxed, and films are shown here under the stars. Past a pebble beach and the belvedere where Marshal Marmont, the French governor, is supposed to have enjoyed a game of cards, St. Mark's Tower watches over a few rowing-boats.

Trogir cathedral's main portal, carved in 13th century, is the artistic highlight of a gem of a town.

SPLIT*

The narrow streets of Split reveal the most astonishing array of historic details: an Egyptian sphinx, a Roman temple, Byzantine lions, Romanesque arches and Renaissance windows. The focus of it all is a colossal ancient palace fit for an emperor.

With a population of a quarter million or so, this busy port is Dalmatia's fastest-growing city. Split's imposing setting in no way inhibits the vigorous, gregarious people who live here.

The city is stretched across a peninsula with harbours on either side—one mainly for pleasure craft, the other Yugoslavia's second-busiest seaport. Above the roofs of the old town rises the campanile of the cathedral. Behind, tall buildings glisten white against the blue haze of the Kozjak and Mosor mountains. Overlooking town and harbour, on the western tip of the peninsula, is wooded Marjan Hill.

The Roman Emperor Diocletian was born in neighbouring Salona, so this was his sentimental choice for a retirement address. It took ten years to build, but when he abdicated in A.D. 305 a palace as big as his ego awaited him. In the 7th century, barbarian tribes devastated Salo-na, whose inhabitants took refuge within the palace walls. In the manner of uninvited guests anywhere, they never left. They also left their mark, partitioning off the vast imperial apartments for their more modest needs.

During the following centuries, Split recognized in turn the sovereignty of the Byzantine empire, the medieval Croatian state and the Croato-Hungarian kings. In

---

* For further details about the Split area, refer to the Berlitz travel guide SPLIT AND DALMATIA.

1420 the city came under Venetian dominion, but it still had to contend with the Turks, who surrounded Split for the next three centuries. Forced to concentrate all its energies on defence, Split declined. The Austrians took over in 1797 and,

In Diocletian's Palace, visitors find the time and place for a drink.

except for a Napoleonic interim, held on until the end of World War I.

Through every adversity, the people of Split have always been intensely independent, proud of any show of local spirit. In World War II, the city's most popular soccer team, almost to a man, joined Tito's partisans.

Many visitors have wandered through Split looking for its su-

preme tourist attraction, only to learn they were already *in* it. For **Diocletian's Palace** (*Dioklecijanova Palača*) is not so much a palace as an ancient walled town. Over the centuries new buildings have been tacked on, inner walls torn down, arches walled up. It's a ruin to revel in, and discover. Don't worry about getting lost in the narrow alleys; they all lead back to civilization, ancient or modern.

As you stroll along the waterfront you can see the palace's colonnade above the shops now embedded in the noble walls. The spaces between the original free-standing columns have been filled in. Halfway along, the Bronze Gate (*Mjedena vrata*) leads down to the **cellars,** vaulted halls directly below the imperial apartments. They indicate the dimensions of the luxury that ruled above stairs. The underground maze is just the place for local children to play hide-and-seek, noisily, with none of the awe foreigners attach to the antiquity around them. The arcade leading to the cellars has been turned into a souvenir shopping centre, bathed in pop music Diocletian couldn't have imagined.

A flight of steps goes up to the **peristyle,** a formal courtyard bordered on three sides by immense Corinthian columns. The fourth side opens onto the intersection of the palace's two main streets.

This majestic precinct, where petitioners used to cringe before the ex-emperor, is now occupied by café tables. You may even hear live jazz, as musicians entertain the crowd.

A black sphinx from ancient Egypt guards the entrance to the emperor's mausoleum, latterly the cathedral of **St. Domnius** (*Sveti Dujam*). Remarkable among the 13th-century features are the painstakingly carved doors, illustrating the life of Christ, and Dalmatia's oldest choir stalls. (Look closely for the signature, in the form of a miniature relief of the sculptor at work.) As a reminder of the building's original purpose, images of Emperor Diocletian and his consort gaze down from medallions in the frieze below the dome.

Outside, again, an alley leads to a small temple, probably dedicated to Jupiter. All that remains is the sanctuary, which early Christians turned into a **baptistery.** On guard before its handsome portal is another sphinx of black granite, this one headless. The central stone slab on the baptismal font (11th century) shows a Croatian king seated on his throne. Behind the font is a bronze statue of St. John the

Older than the palace, an Egyptian sphinx guards the cathedral.

Baptist by Ivan Meštrović. The rather stark interior is vaulted by an elaborate, coffered ceiling.

Along the east side of Diocletian's Palace, beyond the souvenir stalls, bubbles a Mediterranean sort of **market,** though you wouldn't expect to find barrels of sauerkraut (legacy of the Austro-Hungarian empire) in Naples or Nice. This is the busiest place in town starting at sun-up.

Just outside the palace's northern Golden Gate *(Zlatna vrata)* stands a huge bronze **statue** by Meštrović. The fierce-looking subject: a 10th-century bishop, Gregory of Nin, remembered as a Croatian patriot and defender of Slavic culture.

On the west side of the palace, the Iron Gate *(Žetjezna vrata)* leads to Narodni trg (National Square). Young and old congregate here for the early-evening walkabout, which extends as far as the waterfront promenade. You can hear the hum of spirited conversation a street away.

On the tower high above the gate, an unusual clock tells time in Roman numerals. The triple-arched loggia opposite belongs to the old town hall, today the **Ethnographic Museum** *(Etnografski muzej).* Its exhibits include jewellery, fishing paraphernalia and regional costumes; some of the men's outfits are as intricate and flashy as a Spanish bullfighter's "suit of lights".

The ubiquitous Ivan Meštrović turns up again in the middle of Trg Preporoda (Renaissance Square) with a statue of Marko Marulić (1450-1524), a Croatian poet who warned Europe of the Ottoman threat. The Palača Milesi, jutting into the square, has a **Maritime Museum** stowed

---

Dalmatian Whittler

When Ivan Meštrović was growing up in the Dalmatian mountains, the young shepherd carved wood and stone to pass the time. Today his sculptures are considered modern classics. They include Belgrade's Unknown Soldier's Monument and Chicago's statue of an Indian on horseback.

At 15 Meštrović was apprenticed to a master mason in Split. After art school in Vienna he opened a studio in Paris. From an early Impressionist style influenced by Rodin, he developed the distinctive, monumental realism of his mature work. After World War II Meštrović moved to the United States, teaching at Syracuse and Notre Dame universities. He died, a naturalized American citizen, in South Bend, Indiana, in 1962.

The Meštrović Gallery in Split (at Šetalište Moše Pijade 44) gathers under one roof a representative sampling of his prolific body of work in wood, marble and bronze.

84

away upstairs. Here you can see Europe's oldest sailing boat, or at least an illustration of it, from a 4,000-year-old pot fragment discovered on the island of Hvar.

Split has several beaches—the best known is Bačvice. But for a change of scene, head for **Marjan**, the wooded hill where Diocletian hunted. The view of the city and the islands is worth the climb. There's also a small zoo.

Excursions from Split

One popular day-trip for tourists takes in the ruins of ancient **Salona** (near Solin). Soon after you leave Split, the arches of a Roman aqueduct come into view. Originally built to supply the emperor's palace, and restored in the 19th century, the aqueduct still carries water from the River Jadro into Split.

Salona was the most important town in Roman Dalmatia, with an arena, theatre, temples and baths. In a burst of early Christian fervour, 30 churches were added. However, the marauding Avars and Slavs put the towns-people to flight in 614. For centuries after, the abandoned site was a huge quarry of stone, with building material free for the taking.

Meštrović statue of the 10th-century Croatian bishop, Gregory of Nin.

Scattered over a wide slope amid the foundations of basilicas lie tilted sarcophagi, broken columns and fragments of stone doorways. The view from here, a panorama of metropolitan Split's high-rise housing projects, is unlikely to inspire artists or poets.

Another excursion destination, the fortress of **Klis** (9 kilometres—6 miles—from Split) guards a pass between the Kozjak and Mosor mountains. This seems a textbook example of an invulnerable fort. From here you could sight enemy troops several kilometres away, wait for their arrival at the bottom of the bluff, and pour boiling oil straight down on their heads. While waiting for action, the defenders would have enjoyed an engaging view from the ramparts: a happy green valley extending between suburban Split and the hard-hearted karst mountain.

Hills and rugged mountains hem in the pleasant port of Makarska.

> ### A Shallow Beauty
> The Adriatic is one of the world's more shallow seas, averaging only 57 fathoms (104 metres or 342 feet) in depth. By contrast, the bottom of the Pacific Ocean reaches a profound 6,000 fathoms in places.
>
> With a high salt content and a scarcity of plankton, the Adriatic is miraculously transparent. You can spot a fish from afar. Maximum recorded under-Adriatic visibility: nearly 55 metres (180 feet).
>
> For centuries the Slavic name for the Adriatic has been Jadran. Eureka! Now you know why so many hotels, restaurants and cafés along the coast are called Jadran.

Towards Dubrovnik

South-eastwards from Split the dependable but often overcrowded Adriatic Highway parallels the coast, endowed with some inviting beaches. The **Makarska riviera** is the local name for a row of smallish resorts up and down the shore from the attractive port town of **Makarska.** A thriving resort, Makarska follows the curve of a horseshoe bay, where dense pine woods border a most popular beach. Always a presence just inland, the Biokovo mountains rise into mercilessly barren crags and fissures.

Just beyond the port of Kradeljevo the highway skirts a footnoteworthy resort called **Neum.** In a political compromise splitting the Croatian coast asunder, Neum provides the republic of Bosnia-Hercegovina with an outlet to the sea. It's so small, with hills so steep, that the hotels are packed closely together like a proletarian version of Monte Carlo.

Seafood lovers should consider a brief detour to **Ston,** where vast schools of oysters are raised in a pretty inlet as calm and clear as a lake. Nothing fancy here: the succulent bivalves are served on the half-shell, unadorned but for a slice of lemon.

The promising tourist area of **Slano,** with its clean pebble beaches, exploits a deeply indented bay neatly protected from stormy weather. The local folk collect wild herbs. They disperse into the hills to gather laurel, sage, wormwood and other valuable medicinal plants.

The hamlet of **Trsteno** is noted for its formal garden. Laid out in the 16th century, this array of

bamboo, cactus, eucalyptus and oleander is known simply as the Arboretum. The Yugoslavian Academy of Sciences and Arts looks after it. Along the road nearby you can pay your respects to a pair of gargantuan 400-year-old plane trees.

Cameraman strains for a new slant on the charms of Dubrovnik.

DUBROVNIK*

Only a heart of stone could be untouched by this sea-splashed "poem in stone". Preserved behind unconquered walls, the magnificent city of cold marble is ingenious and impeccable. These perfect plazas, these car-less, neon-free streets may look like the set for an epic film, but Dubrovnik is real, and alive.

The venerable city-state evolved its independence under foreign influence—first Byzantine, then Venetian, later Croato-Hungarian. In the 14th century the city, then known as Ragusa, minted its own currency. In the 15th it abolished slavery, inaugurated social services and began wily diplomatic forays. In exchange for heavy payoffs, the Ottoman empire tolerated Dubrovnik's commercial monopoly between east and west. Admiration or envy of the tiny republic's mercantile achievements created the evocative English word for an adventurous merchant ship, "argosy", derived from "Ragusa".

Dubrovnik's golden age of freedom and prosperity, art and scholarship jolted to an end on April 6, 1667. An earthquake killed perhaps 5,000 people and

---

* For detailed coverage of Dubrovnik and environs, consult the Berlitz travel guide DUBROVNIK AND SOUTHERN DALMATIA.

devastated many architectural treasures. For more detailed coverage of Dubrovnik and environs, consult the Berlitz travel guide to Dubrovnik and Southern Dalmatia. Most were rebuilt, a harmonious whole recreated, but life was never the same; 1667 is the accepted dividing line between the glorious past and modern times.

The French army occupied Dubrovnik in 1806. The republic's diplomatic agility couldn't save it from becoming a tributary of the Illyrian Provinces of Napoleon's dreams. Nine years later, under the treaty of Vienna, Dubrovnik was handed over to the Austrians for another century of imperial rule.

Entering the old town from the western suburb of Pile, you walk across a wooden drawbridge and through the Gothic arch of the **Pile Gate** *(Vrata od Pila).* (You can't drive into the old city; motor vehicles are banned.) Set over the arch is one of a number of statues of St. Blaise, the patron saint of Dubrovnik. A thousand years ago, it's said, his warning staved off a Venetian attack.

The **city walls,** among the most imposing and best preserved medieval fortifications in the world, have a circumference of about two kilometres (1¼ miles). They are up to five metres (18 feet) thick, with 15 towers, five bastions, two corner towers and a fortress. For a small charge you can go around the entire circuit, following in the footsteps of the 16th-century sentries.

Within the walls there is only one main street, the grand **Placa** (pronounced *plat*sa). The stone paving, scuffed smooth by centuries of sandals and boots, cries out to be strolled upon. In disciplined ranks, four-storey houses, always of stone, balance the street. Their unpretentious façades subtly play down their commercial character. Most shops retain the distinctive Dalmatian architectural tradition of the arched door-and-window combination, a sort of door-and-a-half.

During the day, the Placa is abustle with tourists and locals on shopping sprees and errands. The shops observe a long lunch-and-siesta break during which the city unwinds into tropical lassitude. Towards sunset the shrieking swallows embark on frantic sorties across the Placa in search of supper. The pigeons, sated on tourist handouts, have no such problems. The Placa provides the perfect stage for the early-evening *korzo,* the traditional round of chatting, flirting, ambling and gaping. As night falls the locals

Great Wall: Dubrovnik's medieval fortifications girdle the city.

outnumber the tourists, and the promenade is so animated it sounds like an immensely successful, outsize cocktail party.

A landmark and rallying point at the western end of the Placa is a 16-sided, domed reservoir known as **Onofrio's Great Fountain** *(Velika Onofrijeva česma)*. Onofrio della Cava, a Neapolitan architect, built Dubrovnik's efficient 15th-century waterworks. This fountain, the city's biggest, lost many decorative touches in the 1667 earthquake.

An earlier tragedy, the quake of 1520, is commemorated at the first church inside the western wall. The tiny **Our Saviour's Church** *(Sveti Spas)* was one of the rare buildings spared in the 1667 upheaval. Its Renaissance façade and Gothic interior survived intact, making it a rare example of Dubrovnik's noblest age of harmony and design.

Next to Sveti Spas, and over-shadowing it, the **Franciscan Monastery** (*Franjevački samo-stan*) is entered through a lavish main portal, facing the Placa. The cloister alongside, which escaped the quake, encloses a lush garden with elegance and even a dash of eccentric humour. Note the car-icatures on the capitals of each pair of octagonal columns.

At the far end of the Placa, the pigeons panic every time the mu-

A Dalmatian artist's vivid impression of a local celebration.

nicipal **clock tower** sounds the hour. Blame a couple of 15th-century bronze clappers, in the form of soldiers, striking a 16th-century bell.

Orlando's Column, in the cen-tre of the square, reflects the reality of the republic of Ragusa. In the Middle Ages, government decrees were proclaimed from the top of the column; malefactors received public punishment at its base.

In a city so well endowed with churches, one might be tempted to slight **St. Blaise** *(Sveti Vlaho),* on the same square. Behind the altar, a 15th-century silver-gilt statuette portrays Dubrovnik's patron saint holding a model of the walled town. The municipal likeness couldn't have been more accurate if it had been based on an aerial photograph.

The history and beauty of Dubrovnik are admirably combined in the **Rector's Palace** *(Knežev dvor),* the city's most impressive structure. There's a stately portico and, inside, a perfectly proportioned courtyard with a grand staircase leading to an arcaded balcony. It was designed by the waterworks man, Onofrio della Cava. The palace was the residence and ceremonial office of the rector of the ancient republic of Ragusa. Lest politics become too serious, the aristocrats of the republic took turns at the job of ruling, each with a one-month term of office.

Another graceful building, the **Palača Sponza,** blends Gothic and Renaissance styles. Notice the delicately arched arcades, intricate tracery on tall Gothic windows on the floor above, and square windows on the top storey. This was the republic's customs house and later the mint.

Now it contains the state archives as well as the Museum of the Socialist Revolution.

Behind Sponza Palace, and not far from Ploče Gate *(Vrata od Ploča),* is the compound of the **Dominican monastery** *(Dominikanski samostan).* A church stood here in the early 14th century, but reconstructions after various disasters have left little of the original. The monastery's cloisters retain the meditative charm for which they were designed 500 years ago, with slender arches within arches, a Renaissance well and tropical flora.

Dubrovnik's baroque **cathedral** *(katedrala)* was built after the 1667 quake to replace a shattered 12th-century church. (A legendary blessing said to have been offered at the start of construction by Richard the Lion-Heart seems to have been ineffective in protecting the structure.) Forget the architecture: the attractions here are works of art inside the cathedral, starting with a large polyptych of the Assumption, signed by Titian. A collection of gold and silver reliquaries in the cathedral treasury is open during restricted hours.

Between the cathedral and the Rector's Palace a gateway tunnels through the great wall to the **old harbour.** Nowadays only smaller craft—local ferryboats, fishing boats and a few yachts—dock here, but it was once an

Near day's end, the strollers begin to crowd Dubrovnik's Placa.

important port, shipbuilding centre and arsenal. Huge iron chains could be stretched between the fortress and the 15th-century breakwater to thwart unwelcome warships.

Landmarks aside, spare some time to escape to the cool back streets of Dubrovnik, where squealing children jump rope and old women embroider just out of range of the dripping laundry. Climb the steep, stepped streets at random to wander among the all-but-hidden churches, mansions, gardens and time-worn stonework. Then take the cable car up the mountainside for a thrilling bird's-eye view over the pale tile roofs as an apricot-coloured sun descends into the deep-blue Adriatic.

Dubrovnik's Isles

From the old harbour of Dubrovnik, local ferryboats zip across to **Lokrum** in 15 minutes. Legend links Lokrum with Richard the Lion–Heart. The valiant English king is said to have been shipwrecked here on his way back from the Third Crusade in 1191. Lokrum, still a most welcome port in a storm, is preserved as a national park, ideal for rambles through the pine woods, for picnics and swimming.

Lokrum's abandoned Benedictine Monastery, begun in the 11th century, was constructed during four distinct architectural eras. Nearby is the royal residence built in the 19th century by Archduke Maximilian of Austria, who soon after its completion was executed by the Mexicans he endeavoured to rule.

The closest of the Elaphite Islands, an archipelago stretching to the north-west of Dubrovnik, is **Koločep**. A few hundred people carry on fishing and sailing as the island's ancient Greek and Roman settlers did. Nature is almost totally unspoiled, with beaches of sand or pebbles and thick pine forests.

The most developed of the Elaphite chain, **Lopud**, has been roused from its long doldrums by a mild tourist boom. But the modern hotels and restaurants don't significantly encroach on the island's verdant beauty. The sightseeing targets are a vice-rector's palace wrapped up in a subtropical garden, and the remains of castles, villas and a monastery.

Down the Coast

A string of resort villages enliven the coast south-east of Dubrovnik. **Cavtat** (pronounced *tsav*tat), the biggest and most interesting, is more than just a pretty beach. In ancient times, this was a city called *Epidaurus*. When it was overrun by invaders in the 7th century, the survivors founded Dubrovnik.

Few historic relics remain; the last of the medieval ramparts fell to eager-beaver city planners in the 19th century. But the setting is hard to beat: a cypress-and-pine-covered peninsula, and palm trees shading the seaside promenade. Unlike some of the yachts lounging about at the quay, the waterfront's old stone houses aren't trying to impress anybody. In spite of greatly expanded tourism Cavtat is looking better than ever; the big hotels are almost lost among the forests.

Sunday in Ćilipi: Konavle Valley folk dancers keep alive old customs and costumes.

97

ĆILIPI

Beyond Cavtat the Adriatic Highway stoops beneath the flight path of Dubrovnik's airport. The runway slashes through the Konavle Valley, a sea of fertility beneath the harsh mountain chain of the same name. Miles of vineyards follow the highway; you can smell the ripening grapes as you speed past.

The village of Ćilipi is the region's folklore capital. On Sunday mornings the neighbours, wearing red caps and black and white costumes, dance beside the church accompanied by strange ancestral musical instruments. Connoisseurs of local colour converge from miles around.

DALMATIA'S ISLANDS

By ferryboat, hydrofoil or excursion steamer, the ports of Dalmatia point the way to islands for every taste: barren or verdant, dormant or vibrant. You can sign up for a one-day tour, out and back, or spend your whole holiday on one of the isles where history comes down to the beach. To help you decide on an itinerary, here's an insular sampler, reading from north to south.

Rich fishing and diving await the adventurous at the foot of cliffs in the Kornati islands.

Kornati Islands

From Zadar or Šibenik you can cruise through a strangely compelling archipelago of nearly 100 unspoiled islands and islets, plus dozens of rocks big enough to have names. (Some of the names are amusing or obscene, supposedly invented by the mischievous fishermen employed as native guides by the Austrian map makers who first surveyed the area.)

The Kornati Islands, now a national park, have none of the luxuries of the tourist spots, nor even the necessities. Most of the isles are mere humps protruding from the sea. Some of the mounds look as if they'd been built by stonemasons, with one row of evenly cut stones upon another. The next isle may look tilted, as if the "construction" had grown top-heavy. Often on the seaward side, cliffs rise sharply from the sea; pockets, sheltered from the salty winds, conceal patches of vegetation and the remains of abandoned houses. If you want to rough it, try a "Robinson Crusoe" holiday in a fisherman's hut on one of the deserted islands. A man Friday delivers groceries, mail and newspapers by boat. Daily.

At first glance, the islands seem so unpromisingly bare you'd think they have no past, much less a future. But relics from the Stone Age have been found here, and in Roman times the archipelago enjoyed something of a boom, as the remains of luxurious villas indicate. However, the water supply has never been generous, and in the 19th century fires and imprudent farming practices exhausted the land.

Tourist excursions call at the anchorage of Mir, where there's a restaurant and café and, just over the hill, a deep salt-water lake. The temperature of the lake is always much warmer than the sea, so out-of-season swimmers can fearlessly take a dip. In Serbo-Croatian *mir* means "peace" or "tranquillity", but the Kornati Mir is thought to be derived from the Latin *murus* (wall), perhaps referring to a cliff face.

Fishing from and among the Kornati Islands is famously rich. Sailing alongside the monumental cliffs can be inspiring... on a calm day. But if it's stormy these can be perilous waters.

Brač

People have been living on Brač since the Stone Age, which is only appropriate; the island is best known for its stone. Diocletian's Palace, just across the sea in Split, was built of Brač stone, and the quarries haven't run out of fine white limestone, the island's chief export. Brač also produces goat's

Historic stones and cascading flowers enhance Hvar's romantic mood.

cheese and wine, both highly prized since Roman times.

In the early Middle Ages, the island's bounty caught the eye of a succession of neighbouring powers. Life by the sea grew so risky that ancient settlements were abandoned for inland safety. When the Venetians gained control in the 15th century, fortified communities developed again along the coast.

The town of **Supetar** is not so much a tourist centre as the administrative capital of the island. Aside from a pleasant harbour, the chief attraction is the cemetery, no less. The local stone has been carved into some opulent tombs, especially the fanciful white mausoleum built in the 1920s for the Petrinović family, who emigrated to Chile and made a big splash in mining.

On the far side of Brač, facing the island of Hvar, **Bol** is close to miles of pebble and sandy beaches, plus the only fresh-water springs on the island. The Hvar steamer also stops at **Milna.** Its deep, protected harbour served briefly as a Russian naval base during the Napoleonic wars.

Hvar

Just over an hour by express catamaran from Split, the island of Hvar has no hustle, no neon, no winter. No cars disturb the old town or port; the only noise is the putter of a fishing boat, the en-thusiastic whoop of a windsurfer regaining his balance, and the crowing of a rooster.

Hvar's annual average of sunshine is a generous 2,715 hours, and the mean temperature in January descends no further than an endurable 9°C (47°F). It's been called the Madeira of the Adriatic because of the climate and the flora: palms, agaves, oleanders and bougainvillea in the gardens and parks, and, covering the hills, a patchwork of lavender, rosemary, olive and grapevine terraces.

This 69-kilometre (43-mile) sliver, the longest island in the Adriatic, has suffered some historical ups and downs. It was founded by the Greeks, farmed by the Romans, settled by the Slavs, menaced by the pirates, ruled lengthily by the Venetians, used briefly by the British, ceded to the Austrians.

One of the Adriatic's surest thrills is the sight of the town of **Hvar,** a scrubbed, tidy place of bleached stone houses backed by rich pine forests. Along the waterfront stands a ceremonial row of palms, rendered less pompous by their varying heights. They shape up like a roll-call of haphazard army recruits.

Head straight for the **Pjaca** (pronounced piazza), called the biggest square in Dalmatia. The architectural ensemble is eccentric but fascinating, from a 16th-century **loggia** with elegant arcades and a balustraded clock tower to **St. Stephen's Cathedral** *(Sveti Stjepan)* with its Gothic choir stalls and 17th-century bell tower alongside. The crenellated walls of the old town end at a fortress called **Španjolo**, though what the Spaniards had to do with it remains a mystery. When the Turks raided and burned the town in 1571, the populace fled up the street of steps to the fortress.

Higher up the hill is Fort Napoleon, built, of course, during the French occupation.

The long **Arzenal** runs along one side of the square. Its big arched entrance on the waterfront was used as a garage for galleys. In 1612 a second storey

Dextrous and devout, Hvar nuns keep alive the isle's lace tradition.

was added to house what's called the oldest communal theatre on the continent of Europe. Shakespeare's Globe was built in London just 13 years earlier. The delightful interior dates from 1800.

The 15th-century **Franciscan Monastery** *(Franjevački samostan)* possesses fine paintings by Italian and local masters, most notably a life-size *Last Supper* in the refectory. For the convenience of the artist, thought to be Matteo Ingoli, the fateful table is pictured as U-shaped. In the monastery garden an old cypress spreads so exuberantly that its branches have to be propped up.

The scent of lavender, sometimes quite overpowering, pervades the island. Lavender oil, which is claimed to cure all manner of ailments while repelling mosquitoes, is sold in small vials at Hvar's souvenir stalls.

The road to Stari Grad is part of Napoleon's legacy; the French contributed hundreds of kilometres of paving during their brief stay in Dalmatia. **Stari Grad** (Old Town) was founded by the Greeks in the 4th century B.C. Among the sights: the fortified summer villa of Croatian poet Petar Hektorović. This 16th-century gem has a delightful fish pond enclosed by an arcaded promenade. The Dominican monastery nearby boasts a painting by Tintoretto.

Korčula

Another long, thin, historic, romantic island, Korčula lies just off the Yugoslavian mainland. The principal, walled city, also called Korčula, of course, is an inspired example of medieval town planning. The streets are laid out in a herringbone pattern ingeniously designed to baffle the winter wind and ease the brunt of the summer sun. Religious and administrative buildings in Gothic and Renaissance style give the squares and lanes a serene grace.

Korčula's history just might extend as far back as the 12th century B.C. when, legend says, it was settled by the Trojans. More

tangibly, the Greeks minted the island's first coins. About 33 B.C. Korčula was brutally Romanized by Octavian Augustus, the emperor who rejected the advances of Cleopatra. The rulers with the greatest staying power were the Venetians, who conquered Korčula in the well-rounded year of 1000 and stayed on for most of the next eight centuries.

At the beginning of the 19th century the island bowed to a succession of formidable rulers: Austria, Britain, France and Russia. During World War II, Korčula changed hands tragically. The Italians controlled the island initially, then they were driven off, only to be replaced by the Germans, who held out until the liberation in September 1944. All the fighting cost many lives and damaged historic buildings, but enough has been preserved to make this one of the Adriatic's most picturesque ports of call.

The geographical bull's-eye and leading architectural achievement of the town of **Korčula** is **St. Mark's Cathedral** (*Katedrala Svetog Marka*), begun at the outset of the 15th century. The

Korčula has always produced fine stone and talented sculptors.

island's stonemasons enjoyed widespread fame; this church with its ornate portal, eccentric gables and rose window shows why. The interior reveals art works of historic interest including two paintings by Tintoretto.

Next door on the main square, the 14th-century Abbot's Palace has been commandeered as a small museum, mostly of antiquities. The exhibits range from priceless church vestments to contemporary Croatian art.

At the elaborately carved main city gate, the town hall with its stately Renaissance loggias evokes memories of Venetian pomp. Altogether the old city contains fewer than 300 buildings, by no means all habitable. One tall, narrow house—half residence, half museum—is billed as the birthplace of Marco Polo. Although the 14th-century explorer probably never set foot in the house (the dates are topsy-turvy), Yugoslavian tradition does maintain that he was a local lad.

During the tourist season Korčula puts on a weekly folklore extravaganza. The *moreška* is an ancient sword dance clashing in symbolism of good versus evil, Korčula against the invaders. The costumes, skill and enthusiasm of the local dancers make for a memorable spectacle, even more exciting in view of the potential danger of the sword-play.

Korčula has an eccentric claim to fame, in the fauna department. It's the only place in the Adriatic where wild jackals dwell. Fortunately, they keep clear of tourist areas. The island is also noted for its wine, an exceedingly dry white wine suggestive of Greek retsina and called, by no coincidence, *Grk*. After the first bottle you'll be able to pronounce it.

Mljet

Less than 90 minutes by hydrofoil from Dubrovnik, Mljet is one of the Adriatic's loveliest, least spoiled islands. For those who really want to get away from it all, there's an islet on a salt-water lake in the middle of this island, with a 12th-century Benedictine monastery converted to a class B hotel. This island-on-an-island is a fragrant garden of pines and cypress, palms and cactus and abundant flowers. You can walk all the way around it, at a contemplative pace, in less than ten minutes, yet it's big enough for a hundred tourists to lose themselves. The islet rises from Veliko jezero (Great Lake), the larger of two linked lakes, which were formed when the sea flooded Mljet's deep karst depressions.

Prehistoric ruins indicate that the natural attractions of Mljet have been enjoyed for thousands of years. Its first fame came in a Greek history book of the 2nd century A.D. Thick Aleppo pine

forests, called the best preserved of the Mediterranean area, cover most of Mljet, but there are vineyards and olive groves as well.

The island's area is about 100 square kilometres (39 square miles). A large section of land on the western side has been set aside as a national park. This peaceful place is the perfect antidote for the pressures of everyday life... or even the pace of tourism.

Mljet's climate supports palms, pines and flowering succulents.

Mljet harbours a zoological novelty: a colony of mongooses. They're descended from a pair imported from India around the turn of the century expressly to eliminate a snake problem. They couldn't have been more effective. Now there's a mongoose problem.

MONTENEGRO

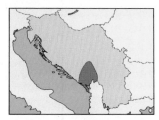

Yugoslavia's smallest republic is heroic in all senses of the word. Here, in an impressive setting, live noble people of legendary courage. Through centuries of hardship, famine and epidemic, of vendettas and wars, they never lost their spirit and pride.

Montenegro reigns over the country's southernmost, beachiest Adriatic coast, which is where the widest tourist track logically leads. Inland, the scene is as dramatic as it is inaccessible: cruel mountains interspersed with inspiring vistas and brave villages. Try to find the time to look at both faces of this majestic land.

THE COAST

Driving south-eastwards down the Adriatic Highway, you know you've entered Montenegro when you cross the language barrier. All at once the signs are printed in the unfamiliar Cyrillic alphabet. "It's Greek to me", you may

despair; indeed, anyone who knows Greek letters has a head-start deciphering the Serbo-Croatian road signs in Montenegro.

Barely recovered from the linguistic shock, you glimpse the stark, cool beauty of the **Bay of Kotor** *(Boka Kotorska),* a world of bold mountains mirrored in a still, blue sea. Bays beyond bays surrounded by oleander, palm and cactus lead up to massive bare mountaintops. The sea penetrates so far into the wall of mountains that Boka Kotorska has a climate all its own—often stormy.

With its obvious strategic importance, this fjord-like valley has attracted the warships of many nations over thousands of years. It has been occupied by Greeks, Romans, Slavs, Croatians, Bosnians, Venetians, Austrians, French, Russians, Turks, Italians and Germans, to name but a dozen.

As the road winds down towards sea level, the first town to appear is **Igalo,** a popular spa once favoured by Marshal Tito. It has expanded into a busy tourist resort and ultra-modern medical centre, but radioactive mudbaths and mineral water still attract the hard core of visitors all year round. Nowadays the ré-

A lonely chapel perched above the cool beauty of Kotor Bay.

gime goes by the name of physio-therapeutics.

The main town on this stretch of coast, **Herceg-Novi,** has a long history as a summer and winter resort. It's popular with all kinds of tourists, as well as participants in congresses and conferences. The highway stays aloof from the town, which is tucked away below and almost out of sight. Elegantly landscaped villas and parks, flourishing in the year-round mild climate, adjoin a quaint walled city. You enter through the main gate, a Turkish arch supporting a 15th-century Venetian clock tower. During the 16th century Herceg-Novi briefly came under Spanish rule. The Spaniards built a fortress, which failed to prevent the Turks from reconquering the town. The Turks rebuilt the fort, but it is still known as Španjola.

The bay narrows to a 273-metre (300-yard) channel at the village of Verige, which means "chains". In the Middle Ages the inner bay was blocked off to enemy ships by stretching chains across the channel.

Kamenari is an undistin-guished village where a fleet of boats provides an efficient short-cut for travellers too busy to circumnavigate the innermost bay. If you're hurrying to Budva or Sveti Stefan, the car-and-bus ferry to Lepetane avoids a long drive. But it would be a pity to miss the sights hidden beyond the straits—some of the most romantic scenery in Europe.

Going the long way around the inner bay, the first town of consequence, **Risan,** was an important outpost of the ancient Illyrian empire. According to Roman war correspondents of the 3rd century B.C., Illyria's Queen Teuta fled to Risan to escape her conquerors. When capture seemed imminent, she took her regal life by plunging into the bay. The Roman connection survives today in some 2nd-century mosaics. You don't have to be a connoisseur of classical art to appreciate the beauty of these patterns, as intricate as a Persian rug.

Perast, a crusty seafarers' town, has been declared a conservation area, a living museum. When Peter the Great was organizing the Russian fleet in the 17th century, he sent a platoon of his young noblemen to the Perast naval academy to learn the ropes. The waterfront and the town square have a bittersweet blend of baroque charm, flowers and nostalgia. The upper storeys of the stately clock tower sprout bushes and foliage, like a distinguished old gentleman who forgot to shave. Just offshore are two small islands. The forested one was always there, but the other is artificial, built by local sailors in the 15th century; its church honours Our Lady of the Rocks *(Gospa od Škrpjela).*

Kotor

Hidden at the remotest, narrowest corner of the most distant bay, Kotor is one of those enchanting old walled towns with twisting narrow streets and medieval churches—but in a setting that's almost out of this world. Below lies the tranquil sea. Above soars a bare, mile-high mountain.

The city walls were begun more than a thousand years ago under Byzantine rule; the Venetians reconstructed them between the 15th and 18th centuries. At some places the walls were as imposing as a three-storey house—no mean feat considering the era and the steep terrain.

Kotor's nautical tradition was launched far back in antiquity. The local seamen's guild has been in business since A.D. 809. And by the end of the 18th century the commercial fleet, known as the Boka Navy, counted 600 ships.

Many a military and natural disaster have marred the history of Kotor, the most recent dated April 1979: an earthquake ravaged much of the southern Adriatic coast, shattering Kotor as badly as any town in its reach. Until the final details of reconstruction have been completed, you may have to rely on your imagination to judge this or that jewel of medieval architecture, still in splints as expert stonemasons mend the fractures.

The 12th-century cathedral of **St. Tryphon** *(Sveti Tripun)* has had plenty of survival experience, especially during the earthquake of 1667 when the façade collapsed. Begun in 1116 and rebuilt over the centuries, the three-aisled basilica is Romanesque with baroque touches. The cathedral treasury contains many priceless works, including a silver-gilt bas-relief by the 15th-century Swiss sculptor Hans of Basle. (This is temporarily on show at St. Mary's Church *[Sveta Marija]*.) Incidentally, there's a maritime angle to the choice of Kotor's patron saint. According to legend, a freighter loaded with religious relics took refuge in Kotor in the 9th century. The local residents bought up the most interesting items on board, which purely by chance pertained to St. Tryphon.

Another 12th-century church still intact, **St. Luke's Basilica** *(Sveti Luka),* has been used by the Orthodox community for several hundred years. Inside the Romanesque building are 12th-century frescoes and more recent icons.

Kotor's best-known landmark, though, is the municipal **clock tower** on the main square. This solid, even chunky edifice, a modest four storeys tall, is dated 1602. After the earthquake it was restored to perfection; you can set your watch by its clocks.

Beyond Kotor, on the far side of the inlet, the only major settle-

ment bears another of those nearly vowelless, seemingly unpro-
nounceable Yugoslavian names
—Prčanj. (Try per*cha*ni.) Here
the parish church of the Birth of
Our Lady *(crkva Rodjenja Bogorodice)*, the biggest in the area,
took well over a century to build.
It's a 19th-century impression of a
Renaissance church.

Lepetane is the terminus of the
Kamenari car ferry. There are
two explanations for the name of
this village. The official story
attributes it to the Lepetan family
who settled here in the 15th century. The unofficial version says
Lepetane is a corruption of the
Italian *le puttane*, the "ladies of
the night" who made this a favourite rest-and-recreation centre
for medieval sailors. Nowadays,
though, it's a somnolent, virtuous
village.

Tivat's climate is so mild that
the aristocrats of Kotor used to

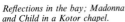

Reflections in the bay; Madonna and Child in a Kotor chapel.

build their summer villas here. Most of the town's permanent residents are employed at the local shipyard, at the nearby airport, or in tourism. From here the highway goes past salt flats before entering the green Župa Valley on the way to Yugoslavia's southernmost coast.

To the Border

Montenegro has endured a terrible series of earthquakes, most joltingly in 1444, 1518 and 1667. When the earth shook again in 1979, all but five houses in the historic fortified town of **Budva** were destroyed or gravely damaged. The authorities aim to restore Budva to its pre-quake glory, but, as the saying goes, Rome wasn't rebuilt in a day. You may still have to dodge scaffolding

113

and brush the dust off your shoes to get the flavour of this evocative place.

Budva has been inhabited since the Bronze Age. Sophocles mentioned it as a "town of Illyria". Archaeologists discovered 4th-century B.C. Greek remains, as well as Roman artefacts. Of the many foreign powers who occupied Budva for better or, usually, worse, the Venetians left the most ineradicable traces. Old Budva was reminiscent of Dubrovnik, though it must be said the town planners here were less fussy about grace and harmony than about getting on with the construction of a city.

Budva's historic highlights are encircled by defensive walls, begun more than a thousand years ago. Even older, the original church of St. John *(Sveti Ivan)*

was reconstructed several times; it has rich icons and archives. In the heart of the old town, the former Benedictine monastery of St. Mary-on-the-Point *(Santa Maria in Punta)* dates back to the year 840. During World War II the Italians used it as a warehouse and stable.

Beyond Budva the beauty of beaches backed by cypress, pine and palm has spurred a rash of

tourist development, reaching its extreme in the master-plan resort community of **Slovenska plaža.** This pedestrians-only low-rise town in white, Mediterranean style is all for fun and totally

Tourism thrives on the beach at Budva; café clients take in all the local colour.

artificial, right down to the *korzo* provided for the early evening promenade. With living and recreational facilities for thousands of guests, it offers all the delights of a quaint native village... minus the quaint natives.

On another wavelength, **Miločer** used to be the summer home of the Yugoslavian royal family. Development here has been strictly controlled; the private park of palms and oleander remains a bastion of tranquillity. The royal residence has been converted into a fashionable hotel.

Just next to Miločer, **Sveti Stefan** is an apparition of beauty deserving the overexploited adjective "unique". There's simply nothing in the world like this charming little fortress jutting haughtily out to sea. If anything, it may be too calculatingly precious.

At the beginning of the 15th century, we're told, the small island of Sveti Stefan (St. Stephen) was fortified to fend off marauding Turks. When the defenders weren't hunkered down, Sveti Stefan did a bit of business on the side as a base for pirate raids on passing ships. Nowadays a reinforced walkway replaces the defensive drawbridge. Today's gatekeepers charge admission of the tourists who arrive by the busload. With the pirates and fishermen gone, the fortress, a national monument, has been turned into Yugoslavia's most distinguished resort. The old stone houses, on delightful crooked streets adorned with pines, palms and roses, seem unchanged from humbler days, but they're all modern luxury within. If you're in the mood for some serious sightseeing, there are a couple of small churches of historic interest—St. Stephen's, a 15th-century edifice, and the 17th-century Church of the Transfiguration. Otherwise, there are perfectly curved beaches on either side of the sandbar. The smaller, prettier one is reserved for hotel guests; non-residents have to pay to use the public beach.

The lesser-known holiday town of **Petrovac** has a long sand-and-pebble beach and, offshore, a pair of islands; on the barren isle rises a fishermen's chapel. Almost hidden in the woods here, a modern pavilion resembling an abandoned café shelters the area's historical-artistic highlight—a large Roman mosaic from the 3rd or 4th century.

The port city of Bar, with a waterfront dominated by cargo hoists and fuel-storage tanks, is of interest to tourists only in its role as a transit point. The car ferry to Bari, Italy, docks here. And this is the terminus of the dramatic Belgrade-to-Bar railway. Another world entirely is **Stari Bar,** a ghost town a few kilometres inland. City walls of

Behind Sveti Stefan's medieval walls, modern luxury reigns.

the 15th and 16th centuries delineate a once-prosperous community, deserted more than a century ago after the Montenegrins ousted the Turks. Among the ruins is the cathedral, which was toppled by an explosion in 1881. Another of the doomed city's churches blew up in 1912. The worst is probably over.

South of Bar a highway leads to the southernmost and perhaps most striking city on the Montenegrin shore, **Ulcinj,** with vivid splashes of oriental colour. Donkeys still carry the onions, eggs and homemade brooms to market, led by veiled women in baggy Turkish pantaloons. It doesn't tax the imagination to recall that

117

this town of mosques and minarets was a hotbed of piracy and the slave trade. You may even sight a few local citizens with African features, descendants of the slaves who got away. And adding to the exotic atmosphere, you'll hear Albanian spoken by a significant proportion of the population.

Ulcinj is said to have been founded thousands of years ago by marauders from the Black Sea. Then came a long series of occupations by Illyrians, Romans, Byzantines, the Kingdom of Zeta (predecessor of Montenegro), Venetians and Ottoman Turks. And incidentally, Ulcinj wasn't finally annexed to Yugoslavia until 1920.

Most of the historic buildings were damaged or destroyed in the earthquake of 1979. But Ulcinj has made the most of the disaster, rebuilding spaciously on the ruins. The big new covered market is nearly as atmospheric as the old, but brighter. Alongside it they've built a modern supermarket; both forms of commerce thrive. Beyond, a cluster of tourist-targetted craft boutiques peddle admirable embroidery and rugs plus knick-knacks of wood, copper and leather.

On the road to Cetinje, the harsh hills of karst surround a fertile interlude.

Four kilometres (2½ miles) east of Ulcinj, **Velika plaža** (Great Beach), backed by dunes and pines, seems to go on to infinity—or at least as far as the Albanian border. This beach slopes very gradually into a gentle sea, making it ideal for children. Connoisseurs revel in the fine sand's rich iodine content. The dunes are endless—Velika plaža extends for 11 kilometres or 7 miles—so picnickers, football players, castle-builders and nudists can all pursue their pleasures in peace.

A Road to Remember

The old road from the coast to Cetinje is a startling achievement of late 19th-century engineering, involving 25 hairpin bends in fewer kilometres. Between mountain terrors, though, there are flat green valleys and stirring views of the Bay of Kotor spread out below.

The old road looks its age, all wrinkled, scrawny and tough. It rarely offers the luxury of a retaining wall, or even a symbolic barrier, on the most dangerous curves. In many places the road is barely as wide as two cars. In this situation, if you're driving downhill and meet an ascending bus or truck, you must back up until you can reach a section of the road wide enough to let the other fellow pass. Not for the faint-hearted.

119

Wrapped in dignity, a roadside delegation proffers flowers.

INLAND MONTENEGRO

The essential excursion from the Montenegrin coast climbs to Cetinje, the former capital of the kingdom, a thoroughly charming hotbed of Ruritanian nostalgia nestling high in the mountains. There are two ways to go: the traditional serpentine route from Kotor, a thrilling experience for the eyes and the nerves; or the smooth modern highway from Budva. For the total Montenegrin experience, go up one way and down the other.

Cetinje

Young diplomats assigned to Cetinje during its heyday as the redoubtable capital of the Kingdom of Montenegro were in for a

the plaque still attached to the gate of the former British embassy: "His Majest's Lcgation".

On a plateau about 670 metres (2,200 feet) above sea level, defended by a circle of the most hostile mountains, Cetinje was, and is, a storybook town. All things considered, the rulers of Montenegro held court with a lot of grace. The official buildings and palaces, scaled down to the size of the kingdom, still stir the imagination.

In the 15th century Cetinje became Montenegro's capital by virtue of its remoteness (the Turks were attacking). It became a theological and cultural centre, and in 1493 a printing press was trundled up the mountain so the burghers could enjoy the benefits of literature. It was Yugoslavia's first press. But a few centuries later the besieged Montenegrins chose freedom over art: they melted down the print shop's lead type to make bullets to fight off another round of Turkish raids.

The royal palace of the talented ruler Petar II Njegoš is called the *Biljarda* because it contained the only billiard table in the realm, hauled all the way from Vienna. This trophy and the armchair in which the mortally ill Njegoš was carried from Kotor, among other fascinating exhibits, illuminate the lives of the 19th-century prince-priest-poet and his people. The tin-roofed palace, now called

shock. The budding ambassadors may have dreamed of postings to Paris or Vienna, but when they wound up (really up) in Cetinje, Europe's smallest and most isolated capital, they knew it was the end of the line. Here in the ever-sensitive Balkans, the European powers felt obliged to maintain embassies, if only to spy on each other. For an idea of the way things were at the turn of the 20th century, note the spelling on the **Njegoš Museum** *(Njegošev muzej)*, also houses an ethnographic collection and an agreeable display of modern paintings. (The billiard tradition begun by Njegoš has not been forgotten here: a big hotel built after the 1979 earthquake provides its guests with a billiard hall.)

The royal palace of King Nikola I, now the **State Museum** *(Državni muzej)*, shows how comfortably Montenegro's last king lived. (He died in exile in 1921 after an unusually long run—56 years—as ruler.) You can inspect the sumptuous banquet halls, and the glass cases glittering with Nikola's accumulation of honours and medals, plus rifles, swords and battle flags, both captured and donated.

Otherwise, just stroll among the pastel-tinted buildings of the town soaking up the feeling of the old kingdom, whose men used to wear two pistols and one sword the way other men wear braces and belt. The former embassies have mostly been turned into museums and libraries. Spare a thought for those ambitious young diplomats facing a winter in Cetinje.

After a long climb, sightseers gaze from Lovčen to infinity.

A most worthwhile side trip from Cetinje, a standard feature of coach tours, climbs to the top of **Mount Lovćen,** a peak of mystic significance for Montenegrins. Nature, art and history meet at the summit, which Njegoš chose as his burial place years before his life was cut short. It's a 20-minute trek up from the car park via hundreds of wide stone steps, finally tunnelling through the peak and emerging at what seems the top of the world. The monument, at more than 1,500 metres (5,000 feet), is claimed to be the world's highest mausoleum; and after you've climbed it you're unlikely to disagree.

The **mausoleum,** completed in 1974, was designed by the sculptor Ivan Meštrović. Two of his distinctive caryatides, gigantic figures of Montenegrin women, guard the entrance. Inside, the greenish granite statue of the prince, about three times life size, is the sculptor's powerful vision of Njegoš the poet, shown with furrowed brow. (His epic poems *Mountain Garland* and *Light of the Microcosm* have been much translated.) The eagle behind him symbolizes liberty. In the crypt below, candles light the marble sarcophagus, inscribed simply "Njegoš 1813–1851".

Lake Skadar

The largest lake in the Balkans, Lake Skadar *(Skadarsko jezero)* forms part of the border between Yugoslavia and Albania. (Three-fifths of the lake is on the Yugoslavian side.) From some vantage points it looks like a big, mysterious marsh. Then it is revealed as an immense, no less mysterious lake.

What makes Lake Skadar (sometimes called Scutari) special is its calm; its scalloped shoreline; its moody mountain backdrop; and the lilies and reeds growing so thickly that the birds can walk upon water.

The Cruel Karst

The mountains of Montenegro, like the mountains extending down Yugoslavia's spine all the way from Istria, are karst. The geological word, inspired by the Karst district of Dalmatia, describes any limestone region notable for its rocky barrenness, underground rivers and caverns.

Generous rainfall is a prerequisite for karst. Slightly acid rain dissolves limestone, creating cracks, grooves and fissures and, eventually, mammoth caves and streams.

Aboveground, the mostly grim landscape is relieved by wild flowers and hardy trees, and by sinkholes in which fertile soil accumulates. Industrious farmers make the most of these depressions, and the rocky desert blooms.

Waterfowl in abundance nest here; other flocks stop by in transit, so bird-watchers have hardly a moment's respite. And the lake is notoriously fishy, so full of trout, whitefish, lake sardines and eels that tourists need no licence to fish. You can hear the engines of the professional fishermen's high-prowed boats droning through the mists.

Like its fish, the lake's statistics are a bit slippery. The depth and area vary substantially with the season, for when the mountain snows melt the lake floods hundreds of square kilometres of surrounding farmland. Most of the historic buildings—essentially ruins of churches, monasteries and fortresses—are found on the tiny islands offshore.

Along the lake are a number of fishing hamlets, but the only town of significance on the Montenegrin side is **Virpazar**. This unpretentious, untouristy place has a lively open-air market. As anywhere in Yugoslavia, it's more sophisticated than it looks; don't be surprised when the man selling pigs whips out his pocket calculator. Virpazar has a modern war memorial planted on a curious knob of rock rising otherwise inconveniently from the centre of town. A coast guard establishment here is out of bounds for tourists. In fact, a sign on the wire fence warns that foreigners may neither watch nor enter.

Titograd

Whereas the old capital of Montenegro, Cetinje, looks backwards wistfully, the new one concentrates on the present and future. Titograd (formerly named Podgorica) has its share of history, but earthquakes over the centuries and almost total devastation in World War II have left little to show for it.

Most of Yugoslavia's inland

towns and cities are built on rivers. Titograd, overendowed, is watered by five of them—the noble Morača, the Zeta, the Ribnica, the Cijevna and the Sitnica. This situation calls for a lot of bridges and riverside parks.

Totally rebuilt after the war, Titograd spread out into the countryside. There's room enough for vast outdoor cafés, boulevards and parking areas; if you're driving you'll rejoice to discover the only sizable city in Yugoslavia where the traffic and parking are no problem.

Titograd is an industrial city of about 130,000, with more than its

Between Yugoslavia and Albania, the mysteries of Lake Skadar.

share of modern office buildings belonging to the municipality, the government of the Montenegrin republic, the university and various enterprises. For most tourists it's a convenient layover on the way to Belgrade, Budva or even Albania. If you're there in late afternoon, drift to ulica Slobode (Freedom Street), the main drag, as thousands of townsfolk do, for the *korzo*. Towards sunset the street is closed to cars so that the multitudes can stroll and chat and gawk, perchance to flirt: a spontaneous promenade, fashion show and street party to which everyone is invited.

If it's history you're looking for, visit the ruins of Doclea, a Roman town a couple of kilometres outside Titograd. Doclea was mentioned by Ptolemy in the 2nd century B.C., but by the 7th century A.D. it seems to have been destroyed. When the town prospered as a provincial capital of the Roman empire, it had all the symbols of its importance. Archaeologists have discovered ramparts, a forum, a triumphal arch, a basilica, villas and, of course, Roman baths.

North from Titograd

The main highway north from Titograd towards Belgrade offers winning scenery of forested mountains giving way to cliffs, confining the rushing, emerald green River Morača. These tre-

mendous glimpses of the **Morača Gorge** *(Kanjon Morače)* are interspersed with many a dark tunnel, but it's a fine introduction to the great outdoors.

Most of the ancient monasteries in the hills of Yugoslavia are rather difficult to reach; they were built in aloof, isolated places, not only to encourage contemplation but to provide extra security during eras of strife. In a valley near Morača Gorge, however, a significant monastery stands right beside the busy road. You won't need hiking shoes.

Established in 1252, **Manastir Morača** found its accessibility a disadvantage in the 15th century when it was all but wiped out during one of the Turkish offensives. (Some of the original frescoes—scenes from the life of Elijah—have been preserved in the Church of the Assumption.) Rebuilt in the 16th century, the monastery acquired some admirable new wall paintings and icons, done by teams of artists assembled here.

If you're heading north, Morača is likely to be the first Orthodox monastery you encounter. Hundreds more, including some world-renowned monuments of art, are scattered over southern Yugoslavia, mostly in Serbia, Kosovo and Macedonia. Their natural settings, the architecture, the frescoes and icons are all so beautiful that you may be inspired to take any number of detours from the more trodden tourist track.

Since 1978 the area around **Mount Durmitor**, much fought over during the war, has been a national park. This is a glorious unspoiled region of pine, beech and maple forests and glacial lakes, a setting bound to impress the most demanding hunter, fisherman, hiker or skier. It also contains Europe's answer to the Grand Canyon.

The recreational capital of the area is the town of **Žabljak**, at an altitude above 1,450 metres (4,700 feet), one of Montenegro's up-and-coming tourist destinations. Headquarters of a national park, it has cheerful modern hotels and motels and private accommodation for the overflow. A handful of summer hikers and mountain climbers were the first tourists to discover Žabljak's attractions. In 1943 Marshal Tito and some of his partisans had less frivolous reasons to explore the region. A memorial tablet marks Tito's Cave, occupied during the Fifth Offensive.

More recently, Žabljak's potential as a winter resort has been appreciated; almost overnight, hotels with a thousand beds were built. For skiers the lure is uncrowded lifts more than après-ski frills. It's still a mountain wonderland in summer, too.

A paved road goes from Žabljak to the shore of **Crno jezero** (Black Lake), a deliciously transparent glacial lake surrounded by forests. In springtime, when the snows melt, water roars into the lake from waterfalls formed at the spur of the moment. Because of the region's porous limestone foundation, the water level drops appreciably as the months go by.

Durmitor's scenic climax is the valley of the River Tara, called Europe's deepest, narrowest river valley. The **Tara Gorge** *(Kanjon Tare)* looks nothing like America's Grand Canyon, to which it is often compared. Here the scenery is lavishly green, and even the imposing cliff walls are adorned with patches of moss, ferns, grass and bushes. The rushing waters of the river are green, too, and crystal clear, except where they are foaming white.

Adventurous tourists with three days to spare can sign up for raft expeditions on the Tara. Each raft, constructed of a dozen big logs, is manoeuvred by an experienced two-man crew through calm pools alternating with churning rapids. Nights are spent ashore in tents; the raft crewmen worry about the cooking. One stretch of rapids is so hair-raising that any tourists who feel queasy about it are invited to walk a short distance along the shore before rejoining the party. But much of the voyage is peacefully awe-inspiring.

NORTHERN YUGOSLAVIA

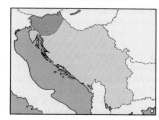

Like a microcosm of Europe, Yugoslavia copes with its own north-south divide. The north is richer than the south. The northerners tend to be more energetic, the southerners, well, easy-going.

This chapter on northern Yugoslavia considers the interior of the republic of Slovenia, plus a section of Croatia. Sometimes the scenery and the characters in the foreground look as if they've been transplanted from the other side of the frontier, from Austria or Hungary. But the people, eminently Slavic, are profoundly different from their neighbours.

Slovenia (population around two million), a republic of fertile landscapes, stylish ski resorts and spas, advertises itself as the "Sunny Side of the Alps". We begin in Ljubljana, the Slovenian capital, a city with the Alps on its horizon, and the kind of architectural advantages that Vienna and Budapest made famous.

LJUBLJANA

The skyscrapers of Ljubljana are a mixed bag; history will judge their aesthetic merits. But regardless of your opinion of the design, there's no argument about their significance: the flashy modernistic buildings reflect an industrious city of more than 300,000 people on the move. If the new tower blocks should leave you unimpressed, concentrate on the old part of town, where the timeless values are defended by ranks of fine baroque houses and churches.

Standing astride all the most vital trade and military routes, Ljubljana is one of those crossroads towns that seems to have been populated forever. In ancient times people lived in stilt houses when the place was mostly a marsh. That was long before the Romans arrived to build an army outpost, which became a city. Not much was left after the Huns roared through in the 5th century.

From the 14th century until after World War I, with brief interruptions, Ljubljana belonged to the Austro-Hungarian empire. That explains the elegant

Real-life celebration: wedding guests in Ljubljana take to the historic cobbled streets.

old buildings and cultural traditions. Ljubljana has been going to the opera since 1660; the Slovenian Philharmonic Society dates back to 1701, a couple of centuries before the foundation of the London Symphony Orchestra.

In World War II Ljubljana was such a spirited centre of resistance that the Germans deported 6,000 citizens and quarantined the rest. They ringed the whole city with 34 kilometres (21 miles) of barbed wire. But the ugly insulation failed to contain the people's defiance, and fighters of the underground intensified the struggle against the occupation forces.

The narrow River Ljubljanica curves through the heart of town, where it is crossed by **Tromostovje,** a gem of a three-pronged stone bridge—the middle route

for motor traffic, with pedestrians to either side. North-west of the bridge, **Prešernov trg,** the city's liveliest square, is named after France Prešern, Slovenia's greatest lyric poet. Facing the square, the 17th-century **Franciscan Church** (*Frančiškanska cerkev*) is an exuberant example of the Italian baroque style.

Across the river, you can't miss the **cathedral** (*stolnica*), built in a hurry between 1700 and 1708; the cupola was added later. It's full of marble and gilt, and equipped with a most extravagant baroque organ. The interior walls and ceilings are devoted to vivid biblical scenes by the North

Alongside Ljubljana's baroque cathedral, a thoroughly engrossing open market holds sway.

Italian painter Giulio Quaglio. In the 16th century Ljubljana was a hotbed of the Protestant Reformation, but the Counter-Reformation won the struggle.

Behind the cathedral, the open **market** is a daily spectacle, where they sell just about anything from oranges and flowers to fur hats and old-fashioned wooden rakes. Onion specialists offer amazing variations, big and tiny, on the humble bulb, and for enthusiasts of Austro-Hungarian flavours, sauerkraut and coleslaw are available fresh from the cask.

All around the old town are distinguished baroque buildings with fading red, yellow or green paint; the district might have a melancholy air if the people weren't so lively. The **Town Hall** (*Magistrat*), with a clock tower on top and a heroic fountain in front, attained its present form in the 18th century. Firmly installed on a hilltop behind the Town Hall is the **castle** (*grad* in Slovenian; but note that elsewhere in Yugoslavia *grad* means city). The sprawling castle dates from the 12th century, though the Romans, and probably prehistoric settlers, were here first. It had to be rebuilt several times, especially after an earthquake in 1511. The castle's greatest asset is the view back down to town and to the distant mountains.

On the other side of the river are the busiest shopping streets. The consumer economy ticks over at an eager pace in Ljubljana, where window shoppers can't resist the enticing displays of expensive fashions and the offerings of luxury imported cars and all manner of electronic novelties.

The spacious modern part of town also has several museums and art galleries. Stop by the **National Museum** (*Narodni muzej*) for the full story on Slovenia from archaeological finds to traditional costumes. One of the delights here is a collection of Slovenian beehive art: the painted panels that welcomed the bees to their hives were adorned with amusing or instructive pictures in naive style, illustrating historical, religious or fabulous themes.

KARST CAVES

The most popular excursion from Ljubljana is a stupendous karst phenomenon some 50 kilometres (30 miles) away, the **Postojna Cave** (*Postojnska jama*). Of the thousands of caves big and small in Slovenia's limestone regions, this was the first to thrill speleologists, who were followed by crowds of ordinary tourists. Well over 20 million have visited the cave since it was first explored in the early 19th century. Postojna is such a busy place that the underground railway taking tourists into the heart of the cavern system has a double track. (But there's a lot of walking, too, so wear sturdy shoes, and a coat, for the temperature is only 8°C [46°F] all year round.)

At the outset of the guided tour, you'll be shown a cavern used by the World War II occupying forces as a fuel depot. The scorched walls testify to a neat job of sabotage the partisans perpetrated. Otherwise, there are vast chambers with fanciful names and amazing colours and shapes, and intriguing side corridors. The cavern called the concert hall is big enough to accommodate an audience of 10,000 people.

Beyond the bright lights of the tourist zone, fearless spelunkers have mapped some 27 kilometres (17 miles) of linked caves here. By way of "wildlife" the star attraction is a strange amphibian properly known as *Proteus anguineus*. Colloquially, it has been called a "man fish" because of its flesh-coloured skin and tiny "hands". This prehistoric leftover is what a salamander would be like if it were a blind cave dweller.

An asphalt road leads from the cave to the romantic **Predjamski grad,** literally "Castle before the Cave". Clinging to the face of a steep cliff, it was built in the 16th century after the older castle, actually inside the huge cave, was deserted. According to legend,

this was the impregnable fortress of a Slovenian Robin Hood named Erasmus. He and his cohorts were able to resist all sieges thanks to a secret tunnel connecting the cave with the nearby Vipava Valley. The route was not discovered until Erasmus was betrayed. The castle now houses an archaeological collection, armour and medieval family portraits.

Between Postojna and the Adriatic coast is another cave complex, far less publicized but easily as worthwhile. **Škocjan Caves** *(Škocjanske jame)* have been adopted by UNESCO as part of the world's heritage worth protecting. Whereas more commercial caves resort to gimmicks, like special lighting and contrived legends, this complex speaks for itself. In the biggest chamber of Škocjan the ceiling is so high you really feel at the centre of the earth. And approaching the underground river—not any old river but a thundering torrent foaming far below—you can imagine the awe its discoverer must have felt.

The guided tour of Škocjan's austere grandeur takes about an hour and a half. Although the footing is often slippery and muddy, the walk is not particularly strenuous; but there's a fair amount of climbing. With a constant temperature of 13°C (55°F), a wrap comes in handy, particularly when it's summer outside.

133

Family picnic at Lipica: the foals will turn white after a few years.

⚑ LIPICA

Almost alongside the Italian border, Lipica is Slovenia's happiest outing for children. Adults love it, too. This is the home of the famous white Lipizzaner horses, the breed that stars in the Spanish Riding School of Vienna and circuses far and wide... when they're not pulling royal coaches. Descended from local and Andalusian horses, they are known around the world for their beauty, grace and intelligence.

The Lipica stud was founded in 1580 by Archduke Charles of Austria, the son of Emperor Ferdinand. Of all the fateful events since then the most painful was the era of World War II, when the herd was moved to Czechoslovakia. More than 200 white stallions were sent into exile, but only 11 came back.

The half-hour guided tour of the premises includes a visit to an 18th-century stable in which the most celebrated pedigreed stallions live; swallows roost there, too, almost as household pets of the horses. A walk among the oaks and linden trees reveals creamy-white brood mares with their gawky black foals (it takes several years for them to change colour). Some of the big-eyed

134

"youngsters", curious or affectionate, come up to the paddock fence to meet and charm the tourists. Like the Lipica stud itself, the horses are long-lived (30 years on average).

Then comes the show, a display of dressage and tricks in time to recorded music, the formally dressed riders and their mounts acting as one. The Lipizzaners prance, dance like ballerinas, and share a joke. It's all greatly entertaining proof of their bright talent, and of the dedication of the staff.

Saddle Up at Lipica

Four centuries of tradition are at the disposal of visitors to the Lipica stud. Dozens of these noble horses are available, along with instructors, to riders of all levels of expertise, whether seasoned equestrians hoping to polish their dressage or eager beginners. For people who don't know a stirrup from a saddle horn and don't really care to learn, there are carriage trips through the karst countryside. And children can ride the local ponies.

Serious horse lovers plan their holidays around a visit of several days to a week at Lipica, which has two hotels with room for several hundred visitors. Dismounted, they pass the time in the swimming pool, the sauna or the disco.

Tally-ho!

LAKES AND HISTORY

Fifty kilometres (31 miles) northwest of Ljubljana, romance embraces glassy green **Lake Bled** (*Blejsko jezero*). The view from the cliff overlooking the lake provides almost a surfeit of scenery: let your gaze descend from the snow-topped Alps down the pine-forested hillsides in every shade of green, finally reaching the lake with its tiny fairy-tale island, from which rises a church, built on the ruins of a pagan temple. The picture has launched a million postcards and travel posters.

The lake shore has been inhabited for thousands of years. Tourists have been coming here for more than 200 years: in summer to walk, climb and rejoice at nature's art; in winter to skate on the frozen lake and ski on nearby slopes. Bled's popularity has its good and bad points. Among the pluses are some world-class hotels and well-developed sports facilities, including an 18-hole golf course. An unusual, secluded hotel, Villa Bled, used to be Marshal Tito's summer residence. Among the guests invited here were Emperor Haile Selassie of Ethopia, Kim Il Sung of North Korea, President Sukarno of Indonesia and the men who ruled the countries of eastern Europe during the 1960s and 70s.

The lake supports colonies of swans and ducks, all prospering on the largesse of tourists. Spar-

rows are relegated to the bottom of the pecking order. You can cross to the island by electrically powered ferry or, half as quickly, aboard the Bled version of a gondola, called a *pletna*. Wooden models of this unique craft are sold locally as souvenirs. Ninety-nine steps rise from the lake to the church, built in Gothic and then baroque style; pilgrims traditionally climbed all the way on their knees before ringing the 16th-century "wishing bell".

Two floors of Bled Castle, high above the lake, house a museum containing historic furniture and tapestries, weapons, and an ancient skeleton under glass. The present castle is mostly of 16th-century design.

About 30 kilometres (18 miles) west of Bled is a larger but lesser known lake with spruce trees stepping down the steep hillsides to its shore. **Lake Bohinj** *(Bohinjsko jezero),* a dream of an Alpine lake, is so clear you can count the fish. At the hamlet of Ribčev Laz, a much-photographed stone bridge alongside an old church spans the spot where the lake evolves into a broad, swift river. The church of **St. John** *(Sveti Janez)* was begun around 1300 in

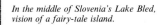

In the middle of Slovenia's Lake Bled, vision of a fairy-tale island.

Romanesque style. Notable are its 15th-century frescoes and Gothic and baroque altars. Hiking paths hereabouts encourage exploration.

For mountain climbers—and more than 100,000 Slovenes belong to the Mountaineering Association—the Bohinj area is a gateway to Yugoslavia's highest peak, Mount Triglav (2,864 metres or 9,397 feet). The mountain is so important to the people's spirit that its silhouette is included in the Slovenian coat-of-arms. Surrounding the peak, Triglav National Park covers nearly 85,000 hectares (325 square miles) of the Julian Alps.

Only a few kilometres from the Austrian and Italian borders, Yugoslavia's best-known winter sports centre, **Kranjska Gora,** usually offers skiing from November to March. In summer the activities are as challenging as hang-gliding and mountain climbing, or as relaxing as strolling through the village and nearby pastures. For sightseeing, there's a 16th-century parish church and a 20th-century chapel built by Russian prisoners-of-war during World War I.

The Slovenian countryside is scattered with roofed hayracks, resembling unfinished, two-dimensional houses. Although the farms are neat and prosperous, you may see horse-drawn, as well as motorized, ploughs.

For an unusual insight into country life and traditions, spare a few minutes for the attractive old village of **Radovljica,** southeast of Bled, where one floor of an 18th-century palace buzzes with bee-keeping lore. The **Beekeeping Museum** *(Čebelarski muzej)* is devoted to the bee's role in agriculture, health and folklore. The local farmers must have had plenty of long winter nights on their hands to inspire them to design and construct bee houses in the shape of a cathedral or a castle, which are among the exhibits here. And you'll admire the comprehensive collection of painted panels from the beehives, decorated with religious, superstitious or historical scenes. In summer swarms of live bees, safely behind glass, participate in this definitive apicultural show. A music school operates downstairs, but the bees don't seem to mind.

EASTERN SLOVENIA

In the heart of **Maribor,** Slovenia's second city, a pious **Plague Column** *(Kužno znamenje)* expresses the gratitude of townsfolk spared by an 18th-century epidemic. The current plague is the traffic, maddening proof of Maribor's crucial location on international transport routes. But don't let that, or the suburbs rife with industry, discourage you; the stately old centre of town is still a good place to visit.

The broad River Drava, so much a part of Maribor, helps to explain the town's importance as far back as the l2th century. And it adds beauty to the edge of the business district. A riverfront reclamation project has restored a long row of worthy old buildings.

Inland, behind the ornate plague monument, a baroque clock tower erupts from the steep roof of the 16th-century **Town Hall** (*Rotovž*). The building comes equipped with a balcony from which the voters in the square below may be harangued. A taller, statelier tower signals the **cathedral** (*stolna cerkev*), which has developed from a 12th-century Romanesque church.

In the morning mist a boatman sets forth across Lake Bled.

Maribor had a Jewish ghetto between the 13th and 15th centuries, from which era a **synagogue** has survived. After the Jews were expelled it was converted into a church and, much later, a warehouse. Except for the eccentric humpbacked roof it really looks indistinguishable from any other old stone house. Nearby, the 15th-century Jews' Tower, part of the medieval town fortifications, is reborn as a photographic gallery. And the sturdy pentagonal Water Tower, right alongside the river, has been restored.

Maribor's **castle** *(grad)* is anything but the stereotype of a castle. First, it's right in the centre of the city; and it is steepled like a church and arcaded like a monastery. But like any good castle, it's very sturdy. The regional **museum,** with old works of art, furniture and costumes, is based here. In the cobbled square next to the castle stands an unusual modern monument, a spherical memorial with startling illustrations honouring martyrs of the World War II resistance.

The brusque name of the historic town of **Ptuj** (26 kilometres or 16 miles south-east of Maribor) may not be music to your ears, but the place is rich in visual charm. (The name seems to be a Slavic version of the town's original Latin name, *Poetovium,* the meaning of which is uncertain. The Romans established a fort here two thousand years ago.)

The whole town is an officially proclaimed historical monument, so it's forbidden to change a chimney or a window frame. It's also illegal to dig a hole without

Starting at the Drava riverfront, Maribor restores its fine historic core.

permission from the archaeologists, lest you unearth some Bronze Age baubles or accidentally ruin some forgotten ancient ruin.

For a thoroughly inspiring overview of Ptuj's seemingly anarchic jumble of red roofs, the river and the fertile countryside all around it, ascend to the **castle,** on a bluff the Romans chose for their fortifications. Far below you can take your bearings from the onion-domed landmark, Ptuj's bell tower–clock tower–watchtower, standing on its own like a steeple in search of a church. Just in front of the tower you'll see the **Orpheus Monument,** a Roman tablet erected in the 2nd century in honour of a local mayor. In the Middle Ages, the slab was used as the town pillory.

Guided tours of the castle reveal eclectic collections of old musical instruments, grandfather clocks, weapons and armour. Note the motto on the coat of arms: "Grip Fast", in English, the byword of a family of Scots, the Leslies, who inhabited the castle by virtue of their service as high-ranking mercenaries with the Austrian army.

In the village of **Ptujska Gora**, 15 kilometres (9 miles) south-west of Ptuj, the **parish church** is considered a superb example of Slovenian late Gothic architecture. The sculptural details inside, from about 1400, are brilliantly lyrical. Outstanding is a **relief** of the Virgin of Mercy, under whose

A personage of Ptuj: a stone carving in the 12th-century castle.

outstretched cloak no fewer than 81 small figures seek protection. It's thought many of the realistically sculpted faces represent prominent townsfolk.

Slovenia has more than a dozen health resorts where Yugoslavs and foreigners congregate. **Rogaška Slatina**, between Maribor and Zagreb, is a striking example of an old-style European spa, to which modern hotels have been added. Everything centres on an immense, flower-decked promenade, dominated by an ochre neo-classical extravaganza reminiscent of Leningrad's Winter Palace. The clients, generally younger than you may have imagined, spend a lot of time strolling the grounds while imbibing the water, which is supposed to cure just about anything. Rich in magnesium, it is bottled and distributed nationally under the brand name *Donat*. As for dieting, watch the health addicts, with their scrubbed pink complexions, breaking parole with ice-cream sundaes at the open-air cafés.

ZAGREB

The capital of the republic of Croatia considers itself the least provincial of Yugoslavia's cities. Zagreb rivals Belgrade for the title of national cultural capital. This dynamic city of industry and parks, with a population of more than one million, supports ten legitimate theatres, a 5,000-seat concert hall, scores of museums, and hundreds of libraries and bookshops. It is the home of the Yugoslavian Academy of Science and Art, as well as the prestigious Lexicographical Institute, publisher of encyclopaedias. On a less solemn cultural level, Zagreb's Oscar-winning animated cartoon studio has given the world many a thoughtful smile.

Zagreb goes back a long way. Settled by prehistoric tribes, it took on a certain importance in Roman times as a military base and municipality. In spite of all the archaeological evidence, the city formally counts itself a mere nine centuries old; the official foundation was chronicled in 1094, when Zagreb became the administrative centre of a diocese. A trade fair, precursor of the modern twice-yearly Zagreb Fair, was held in the 12th century. Zagreb University was founded in 1669.

Not only is the pedigree distinguished; the present-day city is better than ever. In honour of *Universiade '87*, the world student olympics held here, Zagreb's historic buildings were restored, the business district shined to a high gloss and the economic and recreational infrastructure renovated.

The vast main square of modern Zagreb, **Trg Republike** (Republic Square), is reserved for pedestrians and trams (streetcars). This is the place to gauge the mood of the city and start your window-shopping and café-stopping. It's only a little more than a minute by funicular (terminal in Tomićeva Street) to the medieval **Upper Town** *(Gornji grad)*, packed with historical landmarks.

Zagreb's high-flying **cathedral** *(katedrala)* was first consecrated in 1217. It has undergone profound renovations after various natural and man-made disasters, most devastatingly the arrival of the Tartar hordes in the 13th century, and more recently fire and earthquake. This is one place where you can't blame the Turks for all the troubles; the Ottoman army reached the city in 1486 but turned back. The cathedral's twin towers, each telling the time, have soared airily skywards since the end of the 19th century. The bells, the biggest weighing some five tons, carry their tune over much of the city. The cathedral **treasury** has exhibits going back to the 11th century—an ebony diptych, a cloak of Byzantine cloth and manuscripts.

Two other churches in the Upper Town merit admiration. Above a majestic Gothic portal, the roof of **St. Mark's Church** *(Sveti Marka)* displays outsized coats of arms of Croatia and Zagreb in enamel tiles. Inside, there's a powerful, elongated *Crucifixion* by the sculptor Ivan Meštrović and modern frescoes by Joza Kljaković. **St. Catherine's Church** *(Sveta Katarine)*, built by the Jesuits in the 17th century, fairly drips baroque details—frescoes and stucco and woodwork.

The **Stone Gate** *(Kamenita vrata)*, a survival of the original fortifications, contains a small, busy shrine to the Virgin Mary. The walls of the passageway, illuminated by a blaze of votive candles, are lined with plaques of thanks for mercies granted.

The Upper Town's big open **market** *(Tržnica dolac)* has all the earthy ingredients you'd expect when city meets country. Beyond the fruits and vegetables, the last row of stalls caters to tourists, with handicrafts like needlework, wood-carvings and mosaic pictures for sale.

Art lovers head for Rooseveltov trg, where a grand former school building has been converted to house the **Muzej Mimara,** Zagreb's great pride. Here one of the world's major private art hoards, with more than 3,700 works, is thrown open to the public: ancient Chinese porcelain and Egyptian sculpture, Russian and Greek icons, and paintings by Goya and Velázquez, Renoir and Manet. The donor, the world-travelling Ante Topić

Gothic portal of Croatia's biggest church, Zagreb Cathedral.

Mimara, died just before his museum's 1987 opening. Other museums in the culturally crowded Lower Town *(Donji grad)* cover archaeology, history, ethnography and the art of many schools.

Finally, for an offbeat escape, consider a visit to a cool, quiet,

In culturally vigorous Zagreb, a Meštrović statue on show.

historic retreat. There's nothing gloomy about the shade trees and twittering birds in the cemetery of Mirogoj, north of the centre. Wander among the simple gravestones and eloquently sculpted tombs belonging to prominent citizens. Under a remarkable policy, Catholics, Orthodox Christians, Jews and atheists are buried elbow to elbow. Here the last act is oecumenical.

CONTINENTAL YUGOSLAVIA

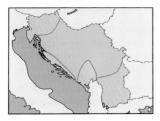

Far from the beach-bound tourist throngs, continental Yugoslavia offers a wide horizon of marvels, as naturally invigorating as mountains and waterfalls, as beautifully contrived as monasteries and mosques. In this land-locked diversity there is something for every taste, and eye, and mind.

We begin on the edge of the Pannonian Plain, in rich farming country at the intersection of two great rivers. For thousands of years this crossroads of east and west has been inhabited, and fought over. It's a commanding location worthy of a capital city.

BELGRADE

A historian, brooding about the variety of conquerors who claimed Belgrade over the centuries, reckons that the city has been destroyed and rebuilt 36 times. This may explain why historic monuments are rare among its attractions. But the modern city of nearly one and a half million inhabitants holds its own as a dynamic hub of government, economy and culture that still knows how to relax.

With archaeological relics going back 7,000 years, Belgrade is one of Europe's oldest cities. Its first known name, from the time the Celts settled here a couple of thousand years ago, was *Singidunum*. The Roman empire soon took over, with all its advantages in culture and public works. Singidunum prospered until the Dark Ages brought centuries of attacks by Ostrogoths, Avars, Slavs and other marauders. In the 15th century the city became the capital of Serbia, which, after many more ups and downs, it remains.

To understand the strategic significance of Belgrade (called *Beograd* or "White City" in Serbo-Croatian), climb to the uppermost part of the much-restored **Kalemegdan Fortress** *(Tvrdjava Kalemegdan)* first fortified by the ancient Celts. From here you look out upon the confluence of Belgrade's rivers. This rare, super-wide-angle picture shows the merger of the junior partner, the Sava, into the swollen inevitability of the Danube. The best vantage point is at the base of the **Victory Monument**, a tall column supporting a giant bronze statue by Meštrović. The monument,

147

commemorating a World War I battle, was to have been erected in central Belgrade, but local sensibilities at the time deemed it circumspect to point the warrior's stark nakedness towards the rivers.

The fortress is scattered with relics of many centuries—gates, towers, tombs, churches, and a so-called Roman well that's really from the 18th century. Only a short walk from the city and its pressures, Kalemegdan is set in agreeable parkland. Belgrade families flock to the fortress less for its monumental importance than for fresh air, shady promenades and sports facilities. Among the historic highlights, look for parts of the original **Roman wall**, plus the 15th-century **Despot's Gate** *(Despotova kapija)*, and, from the same era, the seemingly impregnable **Zindan Gate** *(Zindan kapija)*, as well as the 18th century **Clock Tower** *(Sahat-kula)*. The Turks built with stone, the Austrians who followed used brick, but the ancient Romans built best.

The major landmark in the lower part of the fortress, the octagonal **Nebojša Tower** *(Kula Nebojša)* dates from the 15th century. The name *Nebojša* means "fear not": ironically, the tower, often destroyed and restored, has a lurid history as a dungeon and torture chamber. A modern feature of the fortress,

the **Military Museum** *(Vojni muzej)* dramatically documents Yugoslavian resistance to a sadly abundant list of invaders, most recently the Germans in World War II.

Just outside the fortress, the neo-baroque Orthodox **cathedral** *(Saborna crkva)* looks older than its years. Although it's relatively modest as cathedrals go, this 19th-century church is worth a visit for the atmosphere of calm within, the incense and heavenly music, the beauty of old if not ancient icons and the devotion on the faces of the worshippers. The cathedral holds the relics of the chivalrous Prince Lazar, the loser at the 1389 Battle of Kosovo.

Across the street is the imposing Patriarch's Palace and, around the corner, an institution with the intriguing name of **Café ?**. The original name, "Café by the Church of the Holy Synod", was vetoed by offended clerics. The owner pointedly replaced the censored name with a question-mark, which still stands, defiantly. As ever, it's a magnet for local personalities of the arts.

Here, too, is a multi-chimneyed white mansion called the **Residence of Princess Ljubica** *(Konak kneginje Ljubice)*, now a museum. Built in the first half of the 19th century, it has been deco-

Belgrade schoolgirls share a laugh beneath a scowling face.

rated but not cluttered with valuable period furniture and fixtures collected from various Belgrade homes. Some of the rooms have been fitted out to show how aristocrats in the Balkans lived under Turkish rule—low-slung seats, carpets, Turkish bath and all.

Whether you're looking for the tourist information office, the best shops or an outdoor café, you're bound to drift to the boulevard called the **Terazije** (pronounced with the stress on the second syllable). The area also enjoys lively underground activities, thanks to the spacious pedestrian underpasses, which are the fastest and sometimes only way to cross the busy central streets. These passages, lined with boutiques and cafés, are the only tangible achievement of an expensive plan for a subterranean

mass-transit system, still mostly hypothetical.

The Terazije leads into Trg Republike *(Republic Square)*. You can hardly miss the neo-classical columns and domes of the **National Museum** *(Narodni muzej)* on the square. The institution, founded in 1844, is strong on prehistoric weapons and jewellery unearthed in the area, and can safely claim to own a definitive collection of Serbian art. It includes ancient icons and a 12th-century religious tome, the oldest Serbian book in existence. There's a European art collection, too, featuring the likes of Tintoretto and Rubens, Renoir and Matisse.

The **Fresco Gallery** *(Galerija fresaka)* is a museum full of counterfeits, but don't let that deter you. Here under one roof are perfect copies of the greatest wall-paintings of monasteries in Serbia and beyond. This provides the ideal introduction to the various schools of religious painting before a tour of the monasteries, or the next best thing to a visit if you can't go.

The **Ethnographic Museum** *(Etnografski muzej)* concentrates on Serbia but that doesn't mean monotony; the costumes and the architecture of houses vary from village to village. The museum has a hoard of some 4,000 items of jewellery, starting with startlingly bold designs from prehistoric times. Among the well-displayed revelations are memorial stones called *krasputaši*, which were erected along the roadsides. Some of them feature bas-relief portraits of the mourned citizens.

For another kind of folklore,

Not to every taste: beyond socialist realism in a Belgrade gallery.

151

loiter a while in the **Skadarlija** district, advertised as Belgrade's Montmartre. In an exercise in nostalgia, they've recreated a Bohemian atmosphere in the quarter where actors, artists and writers used to congregate. Originally a gypsy settlement, Skadarlija became the highlight of Belgrade-by-night at the turn of the 20th century; the construction of a brewery inspired a rash of cafés. Cobbled streets, old-fashioned lamp posts, open-air cafés and street entertainers contribute to the calculatedly charming revival of local colour.

Across the river from the heart of town, in a fast-growing former swamp called Novi Beograd (New Belgrade), the **Sava centar** is an enormous modern conference and cultural establishment constructed in stepped pyramid form. The biggest of its 15 halls is a congress hall with 3,725 seats that doubles as a venue for concerts and spectacles. Guided tours of the complex are offered seven days a week. Across the highway, on a roomy, nicely landscaped site, a small skyscraper of the glass-box type houses the party's Central Committee.

The riverside promenade in the quiet suburb of **Zemun**, just north of Novi Beograd, offers lovely views across the wide Danube to flourishing farmland and forest. Through a historical quirk, the old buildings here are grander than you'd expect. For nearly

The ancient game of chess absorbs three men in a Belgrade park.

An Electric Personality

An outstanding figure in the history of electricity and radio is honoured in the **Nikola Tesla Museum** (Muzej Nikole Tesle) at Proleterskih brigada 51 in Belgrade.

While Thomas Edison pushed the development of direct current (DC), Tesla saw the possibilities of using alternating current (AC) to transmit electrical power over substantial distances. Tesla designed the hydroelectric plant at Niagara Falls and lit up America. He was granted hundreds of U.S. patents for his inventions, among them the Tesla coil, used in radio, television and electronics.

The son of a Serbian Orthodox priest, he was born in the village of Smiljan, south of Zagreb, in 1856. After studying and working in Europe, the inventor emigrated to the United States in 1884. An eccentric who got along with pigeons but not people, he died in seclusion in New York in 1943. In 1956 the International Electrotechnical Commission immortalized him, naming the standard unit of the density of magnetic current the "tesla".

153

three centuries while the Ottoman empire occupied Belgrade, Zemun stood just across the frontier, representing the spearhead of Austria and, by extension, all Christendom. When the Turks were finally ejected from Belgrade in 1806 Zemun reverted to its sleepy former character.

On a hilltop overlooking the suburb rises what looks like a frightfully historic monument. Though it stands upon the ruins

In New Belgrade, Sava centar combines conference and cultural facilities, luxury hotel.

of a medieval castle, the tall, turreted Hungarian tower is really less than a century old.

Aside from its stately 18th- and 19th-century houses, Zemun is noted for some colourful fish restaurants; the local speciality is perch fresh from the Danube.

white marble tomb. In a house nearby a selection of memorabilia, including some of the marshal's pictures, pens and pipes, can be seen.

Less than 20 kilometres (12 miles) south of Belgrade, **Mount Avala** provides a shady forest escape on a hot summer day. On top of the 511-metre (1,677-foot) mountain, the **Unknown Soldier's Monument** honours an anonymous casualty of World War I. (Ironically, the monument was built shortly before the destruction of a new generation in World War II.) Meštrović created the ensemble—huge sculptures of barefoot women in peasant dress, representing the Yugoslavian nationalities. Nearby stands Yugoslavia's tallest structure, a needle-thin television tower. Just down the hill, another monument marks the spot where a delegation of Soviet generals died in a plane crash. This happened in 1964, before the TV tower was built; its blinking lights might have warned them that they were heading towards Belgrade's only mountain.

Two Memorials

On a Belgrade hilltop, the **Tito Memorial Centre** *(Memorijalni centar Josip Broz Tito)* pays homage to the late leader in a reverent but unmelancholy way. This sunny, glassed-in mausoleum, brimming with flowers, is anything but lugubrious. An honour guard of soldiers in Technicolor uniforms stands motionless as a single line of citizens and tourists respectfully files past the

The Iron Gates

The longest but most memorable day-trip from Belgrade is an excursion by hydrofoil down the Danube to **Djerdap**, a canyon fraught with natural and historical importance. Cut through the Carpathians, the gorge is so awe-

155

some it was named the Iron Gates.

In the 1960s archaeologists discovered that the region was a cradle of European civilization. Along the river bank they found the Stone Age village of Lepenski Vir, 8,000 years old. The villagers fished the Danube, hunted red deer, built spacious houses and created monumental sculptures. From the excavations, tools of stone, flint and bone, and sculptures (including artistically carved life-size heads) are exhibited at the National Museum in Belgrade and in a small museum near the site; the actual "digs" disappeared beneath the water during the construction of a dam, which in 1972 tamed this hitherto dangerous stretch of the Danube.

A previous engineering triumph here was the completion of

a Roman road in A.D. 100. In an inscription carved into the rock, Emperor Trajan congratulates himself on conquering the mountain and the river. You can see the elegant tablet, labelled *Tabula Traiana*, which was moved to safety high up the wall of the gorge to make way for the dam.

Along the way to the Iron Gates, a splendid sight is the medieval fortress of the town of **Smederevo**, once the capital of Serbia. The riverside **fortress,** built by forced labour in the early 15th century, had five gates, a maze of moats, and 25 towers. In spite of these precautions it succumbed to a Turkish siege. But the worst was yet to come. The fortress was in reasonably good form until 1941, when an ammunition store blew up, all but levelling the vast monument. A 1944 air raid finished the job. After all that, the ruins are still impressive.

NOVI SAD

Seventy-five kilometres (46 miles) north-west of Belgrade, the city of Novi Sad, a centre of commerce and culture, sprawls along the left bank of the Danube. Except for the sweeping power of the river, this part of the country is as undramatic as the flatlands of Iowa, with miles of fertile fields of grain and blazing sunflowers. The resemblance to the American Midwest ends there, however; Iowa isn't known for 18th-century architectural ensembles.

Although it's an industrial town, Novi Sad has an air of dignity befitting a capital city, for it is the capital of the Autonomous Province of Vojvodina, within the republic of Serbia. Visit the **Vojvodina Museum** *(Vojvodinski*

East of Belgrade, the Danube rushing from Black Forest to Black Sea.

muzej) for some insight into the cultural strands converging in this melting pot of a province where many languages are heard: Hungarian, Romanian, Slovakian, Ruthenian. The common language, of course, is Serbo-Croatian. The Hungarian influence is so prevalent, this close to the border, that you may find goulash on the menu as often as *ćevapčići*.

As early as 1963 the **historic centre** of Novi Sad was proclaimed a pedestrians-only zone, enhancing the appeal of the stately 18th- and 19th-century buildings and encouraging outdoor cafés to sprout. The main square, **Trg Slobode** (Freedom Square), is distinguished by the Town Hall, in neo-Renaissance style, and the neo-Gothic cathedral. Both buildings are the work of the same late 19th-century architect.

By way of modern architecture, see the **Serbian National Theatre** *(Srpsko Narodno Pozorište)*, an almost windowless white bunker which manages to avoid a heavy or oppressive appearance. When the original theatre was established in 1861, it was the first in any town in Serbia. Both drama and ballet are produced.

Three bridges span the Danube at Novi Sad, the most recent a novel, six-lane suspension bridge supported by cables attached to two pylons set in the dividing strip. On a bluff across the broad river from the centre of town, **Petrovaradin Castle** is signposted *Tvrdjava,* or fortress. And it's such a thoroughly convincing fortress that it used to be called the Gibraltar of the Danube. (By the same token, the culturally crucial city of Novi Sad itself has been dubbed the Athens of Serbia.) A'building since Roman times, the fort reached the leading edge of defence technology in the 18th century when the Austrians bored 16 kilometres (ten miles) of tunnels into the rock. In 1914, Marshal Tito, then a young soldier, was interned in its dungeons for spreading dangerous ideas. The castle is much more congenial these days, with the added comforts of hotels and a restaurant.

Closer to the Hungarian border, 117 kilometres (72 miles) north-west of Novi Sad, the River Drava town of **Osijek** also has a fortress (here called *Tvrdja)*. Although its walls have mostly tumbled, the buildings within are preserved in their baroque splendour. They include churches, a monastery and, predictably, barracks and headquarters buildings. Local folk spared by an 18th-century epidemic built in gratitude the Plague Column in the middle of the main square. Osijek, the largest town in the Slavonia region, has a goodly proportion of parks and gardens.

PLITVICE

A most romantic and inspiring natural attraction, the **Plitvice Lakes** *(Plitvička jezera)* sprawl about halfway between Zagreb and Zadar. The lakes overflow into one another like a liquid stairway with a carpet of cascades. Although hundreds of thousands of tourists come to share the beauty, enshrined in a national park, it's easy to find solitude along the well-marked paths through the surrounding forests. And if not, the roar of waterfalls insulates you from the multitudes.

The Plitvice phenomenon originates in the karst springs which produce water with a high content of dissolved carbonates. Instead of wearing away the lips of the cascades, the falling water helps to create its own containment. In a perpetual chemical reaction, the water's minerals combine with algae, mosses and limestone to form a deposit which raises the barriers. Hastening toward sea level, the flow changes from year to year, choosing the channel of least resistance at each step.

As if the resulting series of lakes—16 in all, linked by waterfalls or natural tunnels—weren't miraculous enough, the park authorities have made it more accessible if not understandable. Wooden walkways have been built alongside and over waterfalls so you can see the evolution of the cascades from varied vantage points. Up close you can appreciate the extraordinary, changeable colours of the lakes and the power of the plunging water. Of all the waterfalls (in Serbo-Croatian, tersely, the word is *slap*), even the biggest splash is hardly Niagaran. But the cascades are intricately dramatic, and rainbows flit everywhere.

Several hotels overlook **Lake Kozjak** *(Jezero Kozjak)*. You can take a boat trip—ten minutes downstream and 20 minutes back; to avoid noise and fumes the ferries are battery powered, a gesture typical of the national park authorities' respectful treatment of their precious resources. Nature here is undisturbed, yet under intelligent control.

Jajce

By contrast, ecologists might fume with exasperation as they approach the ancient fortress town of Jajce (pronounced *yai*-tseh), about halfway between Plitvice and Sarajevo. A steel mill's smokestacks spew forth a smokescreen that may obscure the tourist sights. Otherwise the picturesque capital of the kings of Bosnia makes an interesting stop for the history enthusiast. And market day (Wednesday) brings to town a throng of the most exotically costumed traders; the big news for visiting shoppers is

the woodwork of shepherds with time on their hands—little boxes for various uses, for instance, and two kinds of flutes.

Jajce's most frequented historical monument is modern: the gymnasium, now a **museum**, in which partisans from all over the country, having braved great dangers and distances, convened on November 29, 1943. In this oasis of liberated Yugoslavia they planned military operations as well as the post-war basis of the nation. Today portraits of Tito, Stalin, Churchill and Roosevelt look down on the simple benches and chairs the delegates used. The event was called the Second Session of the Anti-fascist Council for the National Liberation of Yugoslavia (you'll see the Serbo-Croatian abbreviation, AVNOJ).

Elsewhere in Jajce, a prime ancient site reveals the remains of a **Mithraic temple.** Dating from the time of the Roman legions, who spread the mystical Persian cult through the empire, the shrine contains a dramatically sculpted relief of the sun god, Mithras, killing a sacred bull. Jajce's other sights are churches and mosques shrouded in centuries of history, and the catacombs, an underground mausoleum begun in the early 15th century but never finished.

Walkways lead tourists into the midst of Plitvice's waterfall complex.

SARAJEVO

East meets west, north meets south and past meets present in the capital of Bosnia-Hercegovina, a busy, exotic city of half a million. Sarajevo's skyline of self-confident skyscrapers and historic minarets has something for every taste. And thanks to the 1984 Winter Olympics, for which the town was turned upside down and face-lifted, the facilities—from transit to telecommunications—really work.

Baš-čaršija (the name is derived from the Turkish words for "main business centre") is a swarming, eastern-style bazaar at the eastern end of the long, narrow town. Sarajevo's original market area has been restored to its allure of five centuries ago, when the Turkish viziers held sway. Under red-tiled roofs, artisans hammer copper plates, weave rope and baskets, paint pots. Shoppers find this pedestrians-only labyrinth irresistible for leatherwork, rugs, coffee sets, and wicker baskets big enough to hold a snakecharmer and his pet. After you've absorbed the vivid originality of the architecture, the merchandise and the people, follow your nose to the lamb roasting around the corner.

Close by, a blueish-green dome and slender minaret mark **Gazi Husrev Bey Mosque** *(džamija)*, named after a far-seeing, dynamic and generous governor of Bos-

161

nia, who ordered it built in the early 16th century. The geometry of this complex structure is as elegant as the Arabic calligraphy on the interior walls. The height of the dome is exactly the sum of the length and width of the building. And note the oriental carpets for the worshippers to kneel upon; some of these intricately woven rugs are gifts from visiting heads of Muslim states. The courtyard in front of the mosque contains a fountain and two Turkish mausoleums (türbe).

Just west of the mosque, on a red-brick tower, a clock tells time in ancient Turkish fashion, with sunset marked at 12 o'clock. Anywhere but along the equator this horological system requires constant adjustment, so an astronomer had to be posted nearby.

For another angle on the medieval saga of Sarajevo, see the **Old Serbian Orthodox Church** (Stara Srpska crkva) dedicated to saints Michael and Gabriel, with foundations from the 5th or 6th century. It's essentially a basement church, built to keep a low profile in less tolerant times. Inside, there are 18th-century icons of saints, their faces remarkable for their innocence and spirituality. Although the institution is eminently Serbian, the handiwork on, for instance, the candelabra seems closer to the talent of the Turks.

Across the busy street, ulica Maršala Tita, the old synagogue, begun in the 16th century, contains the **Jewish Museum** (Židovski muzej) With (unusually) English translations of the explanatory signs, the museum's exhibits document the four centuries of the region's Jewish community. (Less than one in five survived World War II.) On show is a reproduction of the celebrated Sarajevo Haggadah, a lavishly illuminated manuscript from medieval Spain.

Despite all its achievements during Turkish times, Sarajevo most quickly calls to mind a 20th-century event—the assassination that touched off World War I. On a wall outside the **Young Bosnia Museum** (Mlada Bosna muzej) a plaque hails Gavrilo Princip's blow for "freedom", against "tyranny". Reproductions of Princip's footprints are sunk in the pavement. They are spread in a dynamic stance as the young revolutionary, now regarded as a Yugoslavian patriot, must have stood poised for the attack. While the motorcade paused indecisively, he fired twice. Each bullet found its target. He killed the Austrian Archduke Franz Ferdinand and his

Tourists exploring the busy pedestrian zone in the heart of Sarajevo.

wife, the Duchess of Hohenberg, igniting the "Balkan tinderbox", which quickly crackled into a world war (see p. 28). The bridge across the River Miljacka here, where it all happened, is named the Princip Bridge.

Another museum, rich in ethnological insights, is the **Regional Museum** *(Zemaljski muzej)* in western Sarajevo. Exhibits include rooms with typical Bosnian furnishings, costumes, handicrafts and musical instruments. In the middle of the museum campus is lush botanical gardens. If you're rushed, simply look at the historic **tombstones**—a few of the thousands of medieval *stećci* found all over Bosnia—scattered about the museum's front lawn. The controversially modern building across the street is Sarajevo's Holiday Inn hotel.

Ilidža

The night before their assassination, the Archduke Franz Ferdinand and his wife stayed in the resort of Ilidža, a few kilometres south-west of Sarajevo. This was a last-minute decision, for fear Sarajevo itself might be dangerous. This case of paranoia (totally justified, as it turned out) was cured too soon. Fatally.

Ilidža is a pleasant, gardened complex of old-fashioned European spa hotels whose guests take the waters provided by the local sulphur springs, popular since Roman times.

Horse-carriages ply the 3-kilometre (2-mile) avenue shaded by plane and chestnut trees leading to **Vrelo Bosne**, the source of the River Bosna, which is, in turn, the source of the name of the Bosnian region. In a lovely park at the base of Mount Igman, clear water gushes to the surface from a network of springs, forming rivulets and lakes which converge into a rushing torrent. Bridges and walkways let you get close enough to witness the birth of a river.

MOSTAR

One of the two or three best-known landmarks of Yugoslavia embellishes the historic town of Mostar, about midway between Sarajevo and the sea. The famous Turkish **bridge** *(Stari most)*, a 16th-century wonder, arches elegantly across the rushing River Neretva. Remarkably, it is still in use, though for pedestrians only—school children, women in black, old gentlemen wearing fezzes, and hordes of tourists.

As the story goes, an earlier attempt to span the river had failed. When the present bridge was under construction, it's said, the sultan, Suleiman the Magnificent, vowed to execute the architect if it didn't stand. The architect, named Hajruddin, prolonged the job for years, but when the day finally came to remove the supports, he fled in fright. He was later found digging his own grave. His pessimism couldn't have been less appropriate: the single-arched bridge (from which Mostar derives its name) has survived all the traffic, floods and attacks. It is Hajruddin's eternal monument.

As you stroll the narrow street leading to the old bridge, notice that each house is painted a different colour. The tradition of individualism carries over to the workshops of the **old bazaar**, where local craftsmen turn copper, silver and gold into intricate designs. The outdoor fruit and vegetable market is animated in the mornings, the produce complemented by fish from the Adriatic, sometimes sold by the fishermen themselves. Downstairs, indoors, is the cheese department. Hold your nose!

Mostar, with a population of more than 100,000, is the kind of melting pot where the chant of the *muezzin,* calling the Muslims to prayer, is followed by church bells. The population divides into three almost equal segments: Muslim, Orthodox and Catholic.

At last count Mostar had 14 mosques with minarets. The most impressive, the **Karadjoz Bey Mosque** (*Karadžozbegova džamija*) of 1557 takes its name from the Turkish worthy who sponsored its construction. (Note that in Mostar shoes may be worn in those parts of mosques clearly reserved for tourists.)

On a bluff above the river, the **Koski Mehmed Pasha Mosque** (*Koski Mehmed pašina džamija*) is somewhat smaller than the Karadjoz Bey Mosque. The interior of the circular walls reveals the remains of frescoes; because of the Islamic restrictions on images, the subject here is floral. The fountain outside is considered the oldest in Hercegovina.

Mostar's churches are also admired. The **Old Orthodox Church** (*Stara pravoslavna crkva*) is actually bigger than it seems; the floor lies far below ground level. The icons, from Yugoslavia, Russia and Venice, date from as early as the 15th century. There is a separate gallery for women. In the 19th century local Catholics, helped by donations from the sultan, put up a church of their own. Soon a **Franciscan monastery** (*Franjevački samostan*) was established next door; it acquired a valuable library and art collection. In 1980 a bright, modern **cathedral** (*katedrala*) was built with soaring yellow roofs.

Aside from the fascinations of the old town, which are many, have a look at the new Mostar, with its well-planned public housing projects—pleasing by any standard, eastern or western.

165

Počitelj

Down the River Neretva from Mostar, the strategic village of Počitelj is even prettier than its pictures. Although it was heavily fortified, Počitelj fell to the Turks in 1471 and remained under the Ottoman empire for four centuries. It fits all the elements of a Turkish town into one small, pleasantly restored package. The oriental architecture, the palm and citrus trees, and the river add up to a scene so appealing that an art colony has prospered here since the 1960s.

Počitelj's **mosque** *(džamija)*, was built in the 1560s. Alongside, its slim minaret stands poised like a three-stage rocket on the launching pad. The *madrasah* (theological school), from the mid-17th century, has a new mission as a restaurant; so has the atmospheric old inn, which dates from the same era.

Medjugorje

Hordes of pilgrims have beaten a path to the obscure village of Medjugorje in the karst wilderness between Mostar and the coast. It is becoming the Fatima or Lourdes of Yugoslavia.

The turning point in the history of Medjugorje (the name means "between the mountains") came on June 24, 1981. Half a dozen local youngsters saw an apparition of the Virgin Mary atop an otherwise unimpressive local hill.

Her message to them, in Serbo-Croatian, emphasized faith, prayer, fasting and peace.

Was it a miracle or a hallucination? Scepticism from both church and state authorities, and repeated interrogations, failed to sway the conviction of the young visionaries, whose sightings of the Madonna continued. Soon the very ordinary local church was overflowing with believers, do-

mestic and foreign. A burgeoning thicket of souvenir stands selling crucifixes, candles and plastic saints could barely cope with the demand from devout package tourists from Ireland, Italy and the United States. The construction of hotels and restaurants made the boom concrete.

Most of the tours of pilgrimage start from Dubrovnik, reaching Medjugorje by coach in about three and a half hours. If you're driving yourself, you're unlikely to find Medjugorje on maps or signposts; look for the market town of Čapljina, from which a good road has been built over the 25 drab kilometres (16 miles) to the prospering village of miracles.

*On the way to Medjugorje shrine,
nuns stock up on tourist trinkets.*

Radimlja Necropolis

East of Čapljina, near the venerable town of Stolac, Radimlja offers a bonanza of mysterious old tombstones. An area the size of a playing field, edged by cypresses, contains Yugoslavia's most important concentration of **Bogomil tombs**. The Bogomils, members of a heretical sect that flourished hereabouts in the Middle Ages (see pp. 26–27), left many unanswered questions. Among them: the significance of the motifs on their gravestones, or *stećci*. Carved on many of the 133 stone monuments are geometric designs and scenes of hunting and tournaments. But the most intriguing sculptures are bas-reliefs featuring a character with his oversized right hand raised towards the sun; standing there in what could be a kilt and a striped jumper, he might just be waving hello.

TO THE MONASTERIES

Serbian monasteries, magnificent monuments of medieval faith and art, are spread far beyond Serbia's present boundaries; some of the most precious are found near the frontiers of Albania and Greece. A group of representative monasteries from the 13th century is dispersed south of the Serbian town of Kraljevo, a possible base for excursions.

Kraljevo, a medium-sized industrial and commercial centre about halfway between Belgrade and Priština, has little to entice the tourist; whatever historic merits it may have accumulated were wiped out in two world wars. **Manastir Žiča,** only a few kilometres south-west of town, also suffered terrible damage—in the 13th, 15th and 19th centuries and again when it was bombed in World War II. After each disaster the monastery was restored, and looking at the smooth, reddish walls today you'd never know the trouble Žiča has seen.

The first archbishop of the Serbian Orthodox Church, St. Sava, made Žiča his seat. This is where the first Serbian kings were crowned. The single-nave, single-dome design of this church is typical of what's called the *Raška* school, which combines Romanesque and Byzantine elements. Some of the frescoes are as old as the church itself.

Most of the Serbian monasteries are hard to reach, on purpose; isolation was good for meditation, as well as security in parlous times. But the sinuous, 12-kilometre (7-mile) road from the small town of Ušće to **Manastir Studenica** has been improved to the point where it is no longer daunting, at least by local standards.

Even at first glance Studenica is simply lovely, the glorious green mountainsides providing the backdrop for the circular white walls that enclose a religious stockade. By far the most imposing building here, the **Church of the Virgin** (*Bogorodična crkva*), was put up at the end of the 12th century by Prince Stefan Nemanja, who united the Serbian state. Even the choice of marbles on the façades is a revelation: striped or waved, the patterns lure the eyes to explore the whole exterior of the church. Some of the frescoes, dating from 1209, are called the earliest examples of a new era of Serbian religious art. The art-

ists don't quite get the hang of perspective, but the faces are full of feeling. This monastery is still active, by the way; to help make ends meet the priests produce their own wine, which is for sale on the premises.

Compared to the drama of Studenica's setting, your first look at **Manastir Sopoćani**, from across a ravine, may be a vague disappointment. Just an old church, you'd think, and obviously restored, at that. But inside you can hardly escape the force of the **frescoes**, with those sensitive biblical faces, a wondrous collection of 13th-century art. The sunlight coming in through large

Innovative medieval frescoes cover the walls of Studenica monastery.

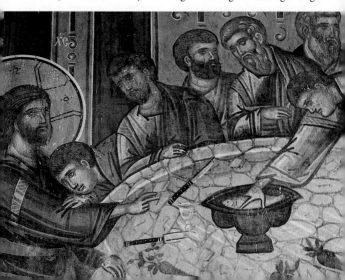

windows, unlike the gloomy scene in most of the ancient Serbian churches, lets you appreciate the talent of the artists to the full. It's amazing that these works survived at all: after a Turkish raid in 1689 the church was abandoned as a roofless ruin for more than two centuries.

Sopoćani is a brief sidetrip from the region's only sizable town, **Novi Pazar**, a mainly Muslim centre with a certain eastern charm. Absorb the atmosphere from the vantage point of one of the cafés where men sit, apparently for hours, drinking coffee or water or nothing at all and playing cards or chess.

The old town—a low-rise warren of shops, workshops and slightly sagging dwellings—provides a jolting contrast to the ambitious new business district.

Novi Pazar was founded by the Turks in the middle of the 15th century, and one of the first buildings to go up was the **Altum-Alem Mosque** (džamija). Built on a square plan, it has a vaulted portico and a graceful minaret. The carpets were woven in Novi Pazar. Also in town are historic Turkish baths and an 18th-century caravanserai.

Before the Ottoman empire ruled hereabouts, Christianity had been firmly installed. Just outside Novi Pazar, the **Church of SS Peter and Paul** (Sveti Petra i Pavla) is one of Yugoslavia's earliest churches, at least a thousand years old. Archaeologists have discovered that the site was in use long before that: Illyrian gold and amber artefacts unearthed here may be seen at the National Museum in Belgrade. On top of the Romanesque church is a curious tower-like dome. Inside, the walls are covered with several layers of frescoes, of which some splendid 13th-century fragments have been restored.

Niš

On the motorway south from Belgrade the full feeling of the Balkans hits you when the direction signs suddenly offer the choice: Sofia or Athens. The principal crossroads is on the outskirts of Niš, the second biggest town in Serbia. Its strategic role on the routes between the Danube and the Adriatic, Aegean and Black seas has been recognized since prehistoric times. The Romans built a fort and then a town, called *Naissus;* this was the birthplace of Constantine the Great, the first Christian emperor of Rome. Since then Niš has been destroyed by many an invading army, most recently in two world wars.

The vast **fortress** (tvrdjava), just across the River Nišava from

At Sopoćani, splendid frescoes survived the cruel centuries.

ПРѢМОУ
ДРОСТЬ
СТВОРИ

the centre of town, was built by the Turks on the site of the original Roman *castrum*. They didn't have to go far for building materials, simply recycling the ancient columns and tombstones. Thanks to destruction at the hands of successive invaders, the interior of the citadel is mostly parkland. The main gate, restored to mint condition, features a Turkish dedication inscribed in Arabic letters.

The most macabre tourist attraction you're ever likely to see is signposted **"Ćele kula"**, on the eastern edge of Niš. Bizarrely, it's right next door to a hospital. Ćele kula means Skull Tower and its opening hours are unusually generous, from 6.30 a.m. to 7.30 p.m. In 1809, rebellious Serbs, hopelessly encircled by the Turks, blew up a powder magazine, themselves and many of the enemy. Furious, the Turkish commandant ordered the Serbian skulls—952 of them—built into the walls of this tower. This gesture was meant to "encourage" the Serbs to stop resisting, but instead it inspired renewed defiance. Over the years souvenir collectors have walked off with about nine-tenths of the skulls; the survivors are now secure behind glass, staring at you.

Candles light rites in an Orthodox church near the Albanian border.

SOUTHERN YUGOSLAVIA

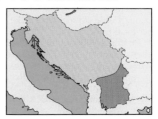

Now it becomes exotic. The landscape of southernmost Yugoslavia is mountainous and often harsh, speckled with refreshing rivers and lakes and timeless villages. The cities, though not as prosperous as in the north, enjoy all the benefits of modern civilization except the rush; when the men aren't strolling, chatting or drinking coffee they are having their shoes shined.

Southern Yugoslavia for our purposes consists of the republic of Macedonia and the autonomous province of Kosovo. Culturally the region is as fascinating as its situation, bordered by Albania, Greece and Bulgaria. Prehistoric artisans left beautiful bequests here; history's gift is an array of magnificent monasteries and mosques. When you're tired of sightseeing, there's plenty of boating, fishing, skiing and shopping.

PRIŠTINA

The capital of Kosovo has risen rapidly to big-city stature, with a population above 200,000 and enough little skyscrapers to flatter local pride.

Priština has been inhabited for thousands of years. The **Kosovo Museum** *(Kosovski muzej)*, exploiting the prehistoric potential, has acquired some enviable works of Stone Age art. A figurine close to 5,000 years old portrays a sloe-eyed personage, perhaps a deity, enthroned with hands on hips. The museum's collection of sculpture, pottery and jewellery covers the ages of Greece and Rome and on through Turkish times. But note that visitors in various seasons have reported the museum closed for renovations, or just closed.

The **Imperial Mosque** *(Fatih džamija)*, Priština's most imposing historic building, was built in 1461 under the intellectual but harsh Sultan Mohammed II (the Conqueror). At the time, its dome—more than 13 metres (44 feet) in diameter—was an extravagant achievement. Near the mosque's tapering minaret stands a stately clock tower, only about a century old. Opposite the mosque, a distinguished old Turkish house with a jutting balcony has been preserved.

The big event of the day, every day, in Priština is the *korzo*, the traditional early-evening promenade, when young people come out to see and be seen while the older generation catches up on all the gossip. Even dressed in black, the girls of Kosovo are notoriously beautiful; many of the young men are as tall as basketball players. Thinking big, the town fathers close the whole main avenue, Maršala Tita, from 6 to 10 p.m., creating enough strolling space to exhaust the most dedicated hiker.

Just Outside Priština

One of history's epic battles took place on the **Field of Kosovo** *(Kosovo Polje)*. There, on June 28, 1389, a vast Turkish army, under Sultan Murad I, destroyed the valiant Serbian defenders, led by Prince Lazar. Both leaders were slain on the battlefield: Murad was murdered and Lazar executed. The unexpected Turkish triumph crushed Serbia, breaking down the door to the Balkans.

If you want to absorb the mood of that sweeping historic site, *don't* ask the way to Kosovo Polje, the name of a rather grubby rail junction a few kilometres west of Priština. The *real* Kosovo

Their shoes set aside, the faithful bow reverently at a mosque in Priština, Kosovo.

Polje is signposted **Gazi Mestan**, referring to a tomb on the battlefield itself. More easily visible is the **Monument to the Heroes of Kosovo**, a modern tower patterned on a medieval keep. From the top you can survey the whole field, covered with red peonies.

Scarcely 10 kilometres (6 miles) south-east of Priština, the 14th-century **Manastir Gračanica** has been pillaged by many an invader. Ironically, it still suffers. Although surrounded by high stone walls, the church is the victim of present-day vandals who have carved ugly graffiti into the frescoes of the porch.

Gračanica was built between 1313 and 1315 at the expense of King Milutin (later promoted to saint). For a look at the bearded benefactor, notice the painting of a potentate holding a model of the church in his hands. Opposite stands his demure wife, Queen Simonida, who is also pictured about to be crowned by an angel.

Architecturally the church is an original and pleasing variation of Byzantine-Serbian style, with rising tiers of curved roofs and domes, and a generally uplifting profile. Inside, too, the accent is on the vertical, and the eye is irresistibly drawn heavenwards. Every wall and column is full of **frescoes**, mostly from the beginning of the 14th century, dramatizing biblical events; some of the

---

The Balkan Syndrome

In the autonomous province of Kosovo, which is part of Serbia, ethnic Albanians make up 85 per cent of the population of more than one and a half million. Of the 15 per cent minority, the bulk are Serbians. The ratio is becoming ever more one-sided: the Albanian population is growing at the fastest rate in the country, and the Serbs have been moving out. Tensions between the population groups—Albanian nationalists demanding more power versus Serbs who feel intimidated—have led to violent incidents. Pessimists are reminded of the Balkan tinderbox syndrome.

Against this dark background, the province's historical sights recall less complicated times, when architects and artists beautified everything they touched.

---

compositions are powerful, and faces show emotions that are believable. Over the centuries the identity of the artists has been forgotten.

PEĆ

At the foot of severe yet appealing mountains, bisected by a fast-flowing river, Peć (87 kilometres or 54 miles west of Priština) is a relaxed little city with a prominent past. For nearly five centuries Peć was the seat of the

Serbian Orthodox Church, which is still its prime tourist attraction.

But begin in the oriental hurly-burly of the old **bazaar,** where they sell filigree in many forms, Albanian rugs in an infinity of patterns, intricately embroidered bolero jackets for brides and special little slippers traditionally worn by an only child to ward off harm. The old main street of the market area is now called ulica Bratstvo-Jedinstvo—meaning Brotherhood-Unity Street—an unlikely socialist sentiment in this capitalist-style hubbub. Seated beggars impassively await subsidies; in inflationary Yugoslavia they expect folding money.

From afar the **Patriarchate of Peć** (Pećka Patrijaršija), on the edge of town, looks like a multi-domed church. Actually it's four medieval churches built shoulder to shoulder and linked by a common narthex. The central dome belongs to the **Church of the Apostles** (Apostolska crkva) a 13th-century example of the Raška school of architecture. It's dark inside, but a ray of sunlight may angle commandingly to earth from a window high in the cupola, illuminating the gloom with drama. Raise your eyes to the dome's interior, decorated with a forceful fresco of the Ascension. Notice, too, all the delicate stonework. In the monastery grounds a couple of dozen

Adventures en Route
Driving through Kosovo you have to be ready for anything. A road may change from broadly paved to deeply holed, then back again, and you never know which it will be from minute to minute.

In the villages they have a solidly Marxist idea about the roads: "to each according to his needs". Thus pedestrians swarm into the roadway, sharing it equally with horses, cows, bikes, cars and trucks. It's particularly difficult at the hours when schools or factories dismiss their inmates, who troop cheerfully down the middle of the highway. If you're behind the wheel, keep your temper, don't sound your horn, and hope for a path through the maze of human and animal obstacles. And watch out for irritable dogs who take violent offence at intruding vehicles. Many a village has its noisily fanatical, car-hating cur who loves to bite tires.

nuns cultivate onions, lettuce and honey. A storied black mulberry tree here is said to be older than the monastery; divided into two, it hangs heavily over the ground, heading in opposite directions.

Just west of Peć begins the route through the **Rugovo Gorge** (Rugovska klisura) to Montenegro and the sea. The road, a

challenge at the best of times, is closed in winter. Even a glimpse of the gorge scenery inspires: overhanging cliffs, raging rapids, and terrain so difficult you'll see cows being hauled to or from mountain pastures. At a waterfall, local climbers have built a fountain from which passersby can slurp real mountain water. Icy cold year-round, this is water as it used to taste: as delicious as the uncontaminated air.

Dečani Monastery

Fourteen kilometres (9 miles) south of Peć is the dusty, uninspiring village of Dečani. Don't despair: a couple of kilometres to the west, another world begins.

Surrounded by a stockade-style high stone fence, Manastir Dečani, almost on the Albanian border, is one of Serbia's most perfect medieval monasteries. The centrepiece of the grassy compound, which includes living

Serbian kings were crowned in the Patriarchate of Peć; a turban suffices in the Priština market.

quarters for the monks and an artificial brook, is a magnificent 14th-century **church** built like a sumptuous layer cake of alternating lighter and darker blocks of polished marble. The church's four portals and 33 windows are decorated with delightful sculptural details—saints, real or mythological animals, and abstractions.

But look carefully, high above the west door: one of a huge matched pair of gargoyles is missing. Legend says that during the Ottoman occupation a Muslim dignitary came here on a solemn mission to convert the church into a mosque. Going through the formalities before entering the church, he knelt just outside the

179

main portal. At this instant, it is said, the stone gargoyle providentially fell onto his head. The fatal coincidence was too striking to ignore, so Islam allowed the Orthodox religion to prevail here. In fact, after some initial conflicts, the Turks protected the monastery for several centuries.

The **frescoes** inside the Dečani church add up to the largest collection of medieval Serbian art anywhere. More than a thousand scenes, essentially a picture book of Bible stories for illiterates, run from floor to topmost cupola; you'd need binoculars to appreciate the highest level. During the first half of the 14th century teams of artists assembled here to paint portraits of everybody from Adam and Eve to contemporary noblemen. (The founders of the church, King Dušan and King Stefan of Dečani, are pictured on the upper arch of the tympanum.) The name of only one of the artists is known: he signed, in red, "Sergius the Sinful".

PRIZREN

Since Turkish times a graceful footbridge has spanned the River Bistrica rushing through the centre of Prizren. Unlike the famous

A minaret as white as the snow marks a Muslim village in Kosovo.

bridge in Mostar, this one failed the ultimate engineering test: washed away in a 1985 flood, it had to be rebuilt. The river has always been vital to the prosperity of Prizren, and it still turns water mills. In the middle of town stone embankments contain the Bistrica, but the attempted landscaping is on the wild side: helter-skelter outbursts of bushes and trees grow along the stream.

Elsewhere in polyglot Yugoslavia you may be bemused by signs in both Cyrillic and Latin alphabets. In Kosovo generally, the names of towns are written in familiar Latin letters but in two different versions, spattered with diacritical marks; the languages are Serbo-Croatian and Albanian. It's even more complicated in Prizren, which has a sizable minority descended from Turkish immigrants of the Middle Ages; so the street signs are in *three* languages, and Turkish joins the general babel.

The ancient Romans were the first to develop Prizren, under the name of *Theranda*. After Rome fell, Byzantium took charge, starting work on a fortress. Its ruins still stand, a steep half-hour's walk above the town centre. Prizren was important enough to coin its own money. Overrun by the Turks in 1445, it slid into oblivion, and stayed out of history's eye until the 19th century.

The **Church of the Mother of God Ljeviška** (crkva Bogorodice Ljeviške), begun in the 10th century, has led a double life. Between 1756 and 1912 it served as a mosque. This was bad for the frescoes, which were seriously damaged under Turkish control, but many have been restored to something like their original warmth and drama.

Prizren's prime Islamic monument, the 17th-century **Sinan Pasha Mosque** (Sinan pašina džamija), now serves as a museum of oriental manuscripts. Restorers have given new brilliance to the frescoes in the dome, nearly 14 metres (45 feet) in diameter. Light from 44 windows and a rose window warms the mosque and reveals details of the decorative carvings and calligraphy. To reach the top of the adjoining minaret you have to climb 105 stairs.

Every Wednesday, market day, country folk in their Turkish or Albanian costumes converge colourfully on Prizren. (As an extra complication, Albanian Catholics dress differently from Albanian Muslims.) Tourists who miss the weekly trading in sheep, pigs and cows needn't despair. The town's most exciting shopping is available daily—knives and daggers and filigreed gold and silver, some of it as intricate as the medieval workmanship seen in museums.

SKOPJE

A dauntless survivor, Skopje manages to pick up the pieces after each catastrophe, natural or unnatural. Most recently, the capital of the republic of Macedonia suffered a cataclysmic earthquake in 1963. Then it had to be rebuilt yet again, more grandly than ever. Perhaps too grandly.

Skopje (population more than half a million) seems to have been inhabited for thousands of years. Under its early name of *Skupi* the town was mentioned by the Roman historian Livy and the map-making pioneer Ptolemy. The first reported earthquake came in A.D. 518. According to the chronicles, Skopje was levelled, "as if it had been sacked by the most terrible conquerors". The latest catastrophe, on Friday, July 26, 1963, killed more than a thousand people, injured another 3,300 and destroyed nearly half of all the houses. This time the rest of Yugoslavia and the world rushed in to help.

Macedonia's longest river, the Vardar, rushes through the heart of Skopje, conveniently dividing the old city from the new. Among the bridges across the broad stream is one known simply as the **Stone Bridge** (Kameni most). It is

Skopje market stalls sell everything imaginable, at negotiable prices.

more than five centuries old. Replacing an ancient Roman bridge, it was built astride 14 arches during Skopje's Turkish era. The Stone Bridge was destined to survive the 1963 quake even while the modern structures all around it were crumbling.

Just across the bridge at the beginning of the old town stands a typical yet exceptional monument of 15th-century Turkish architecture. What could be more typically Turkish than public baths? The massive stone-and-brick walls of the **Daut Pasha Baths** *(Daut pašin hamam)* contain 15 rooms beneath two great domes plus 11 scattered, smaller cupolas. After World War II, when the baths were all washed up, the lovely building was converted into an **art gallery.** The atmosphere turns out to be perfect for displays of both medieval icons and modern Macedonian paintings. And if you need an excuse to become a patron of the arts, it's cool inside.

The 15th century also gave Skopje its most important mosques: **Mustapha Pasha Mosque** *(Mustafa pašin džamija),* on a plateau overlooking the town, dates from the year 1492. A white marble portico with three semicircular arches leads into the spacious building, topped with a vast dome. On the same side of the river, the **Sultan Murat Mosque** *(Sultan Muratova džami-*

ja) was built on the ruins of an Orthodox church. Fate had the last word, for the mosque was burned down twice: accidentally in the 16th century and, after reconstruction, purposely in the 17th.

For many centuries the Skopje **bazaar** *(čaršija)* has been an important commercial crossroads. Hundreds of small shops here sell everything from copper coffee sets to sandals to T-shirts. Beyond these narrow lanes, the swarming **Bit Pazar** marketplace looks as if it has everything Marrakesh can offer except the snake-charmers. It's so colourful you may think nothing has changed since the Middle Ages, certainly not the faces, the costumes or the haggling.

Up a hill near the restored walls of the Kale, a medieval fortress, Skopje's **Modern Art Museum** *(Muzej moderne umetnosti)* exhibits works donated to the city after the 1963 earthquake. Among the foreign artists who gave their art in solidarity were Calder, Hartung and Picasso.

The most valuable Christian monument in the Skopje area was built long before the Turks arrived: **Manastir Sveti Pantelejmon.** It overlooks the city from the mountainside village of Nerezi, a few kilometres out of town. Built in the 12th century, the monastery suffered a number of disasters, and it wasn't until the

20th century that the original **frescoes**, rediscovered beneath layers of plaster, were restored. Orthodox church art evolved according to a set of rigid rules, but within them the artist known as the Master of Nerezi broke brilliant new ground. Some of the faces and figures he painted are uncommonly moving, conveying drama and anguish with a perception centuries ahead of its time.

Ever Since Alexander

Today's bucolic Macedonian reality bears but the slightest resemblance to the imperial might of Alexander the Great. Yet pride is undimmed in his empire's Yugoslavian descendant, the Socialist Republic of Macedonia, until recently a sleepy backwater. (The area known as Macedonia also extends into Greece and Bulgaria. The two Balkan Wars preceding World War I involved conflicts over control of Macedonia.)

In the 10th century Macedonia was the cradle of Slavic literature and culture. It's still the place to find medieval monasteries with the most exquisite icons and frescoes.

Southernmost of Yugoslavia's republics, Macedonia can be uncomfortably hot in summer. Happily, relief is at hand in the pine-covered mountains, cool rivers and lakes.

Tetovo

On the way from Skopje to Macedonia's greatest tourist attraction, Lake Ohrid, the mountain scenery never palls: pine forests giving way to teetering pastures and deep green valleys. In the plain, the town of Tetovo resembles many another quaint old place in the throes of modernization. Although the back streets retain a certain dusty charm, the new official buildings and housing projects won't win any international prizes.

See Tetovo's most admirable 17th-century souvenir, the **Multicoloured Mosque** *(Aladža džamija)*, which doesn't particularly resemble a mosque. You might think it was a house of cards, for its exterior walls are decorated with rectangles of symmetrical designs like a deck of playing cards. It's all far more subtle and eccentric than it looks at first glance. The artist is unknown.

Just south-west of Tetovo, an extraordinary, stone-walled encampment called **Arabati Baba teke** used to be a monastery of the whirling dervishes. They might, indeed, whirl in their graves (the adjoining cemetery is well cared for) to see the busloads of tourists dancing to a live band in the courtyard. Except for these dissonances, the leafy compound would be conducive to meditation. The buildings have been restored to perhaps better than

Fish of astonishing varieties hide among Lake Ohrid's reeds.

their original condition. The installation includes a hotel and, in the refectory in which the monks used to dine, a restaurant. (Dervishes, followers of a mystical Muslim sect, still exist in these parts. In Prizren they hold a sort of annual convention.)

LAKE OHRID

For its beauty alone, Lake Ohrid *(Ohridsko jezero)* would be a prized attraction in any part of the world. But there's much more to it than the clear, inviting water and the striking backdrop; the lake ripples with history and mystery and international intrigue.

The historical record goes back to the ancient Illyrians, Philip II of Macedonia, the age of Rome and the flowering of Slavic culture; the monuments speak for themselves. The mystery is the water's acute translucency and the survival of species of fish long extinct everywhere else; of more practical interest, gourmets hail the Ohrid salmon trout. The in-

ternational intrigue is the frontier beyond which enigmatic Albania controls one-third of the lake; you can see the guard posts.

With its own international airport (near the site of the original Illyrian settlement of 3,000 years ago), Lake Ohrid is geared to tourism. Although the town of Ohrid itself has few hotel rooms, big tourist complexes have been developed along the lake shore, linked by bus, boat and a mini-train on wheels; and there are campgrounds in privileged lakeside situations.

If you were to arrive by boat, your first sight of the old town of **Ohrid** would be of a delightful jumble climbing a hillside. The houses seem crammed into an anarchic mob, the antithesis of urban planning, but on closer inspection you'll find it all works. It's a pleasure to roam here. The hanging street lamps are shaped to reflect the form of the elegant old houses, with the upper storeys projecting in an inverted-pyramid style.

At the top of the hill are the remains of **Samuilo Fortress** (*Samuilova tvrdjava*), the headquarters of the 10th-century Emperor Samuilo (Samuel) of Macedonia. The Macedonian empire expanded relentlessly under this tsar, extending from the Danube to the Adriatic; its capital, Ohrid, prospered. But it came to an end in 1014, when the Byzantine Empe-

The 22-Metre View

When the sky above is bright blue you can see a fish 22 metres (72 feet) below the surface of Lake Ohrid, one of Europe's most translucent bodies of water. It's also one of the deepest—more than 288 metres (947 feet) at rock bottom.

The fish you see may be as commonplace as carp or chub or as highly prized as the tasty local forms of trout, letnica and belvica. But the fish here also come in varieties that ichthyologists marvel at. The lake is home to several species of fish seen nowhere else, including some (hitherto known only through fossils) that were thought to have been extinct.

A much-exploited fish is a little one called plašica, whose scales are transformed by a secret process into what's called Ohrid mother-of-pearl. Necklaces made of these "pearls" are displayed by the dozen in the shop windows of Ohrid. There seem to be enough of them on sale to adorn half the population.

187

ror Basil II captured, then blinded, 14,000 Macedonian troops before over-running Ohrid.

The church of **St. Clement** *(Sveti Kliment)*, otherwise known as the Church of the Virgin Peribleptos, was built at the end of the 13th century. It contains outstanding frescoes, many restored to their original brilliance. Illustrations of Bible stories, the life of Christ and the Virgin, go on in a fixed sequence, for instance from the south wall to the north, then from east to west. If this doesn't confuse you, the problem of names may: two other churches in Ohrid are dedicated to the same St. Clement—a monastery below the fortress, and *old* St. Clement's, near the lower gate. The saint in question, a tireless missionary remembered as a great educator, was the first bishop here.

The 11th-century cathedral of **St. Sophia** *(Sveta Sofija)*, alias the Church of Holy Wisdom, stands in the centre of the old town on the ruins of a 5th-century basilica. This is the place to see some vivid frescoes, delicate yet forceful, among the finest examples of Byzantine art. They were inadvertently well pre-

"Liturgy of St. Basil the Great", an 11th-century Byzantine fresco, in St. Sophia cathedral, Ohrid.

served for five centuries during Turkish rule; the cathedral was turned into a mosque and the walls were repainted, thus protecting the biblical compositions from the elements.

Ohrid's main shopping-and-strolling street runs from near the waterfront to a monumental plane tree thought to be about 900 years old. The early evening *korzo* is always an event worth attending. On Saturdays the

young men come straight from the overworked barber shops, sporting identical new hairstyles inspired by the latest film or pop star. They seem to outnumber the girls, who proceed in cheerful but evidently unattainable twos and threes.

Borderline Monastery

From Ohrid a scenic road leads southwards 29 kilometres (18 miles) to the famous **Manastir**

the saint of the same name, who along with St. Clement was a pillar of early Slavonic culture. The original church, destroyed during the Turkish occupation, was replaced ·between the 16th and 18th centuries. Among the works of art visible today are an early 18th-century iconostasis involving complicated effects carved in wood, and frescoes illustrating the miraculous life of St. Naum; he was particularly influential with psychologically disturbed people.

Peacocks trail across the tranquil monastery grounds, now equipped with a hotel and restaurant.

East of Ohrid

Macedonia's second biggest city, **Bitola**, is about as close to the border with Greece as Ohrid is to Albania. This strategically important place, a pleasant, gardened town, has considerable archaeological importance. A couple of kilometres outside Bitola, the ancient city of **Heraclea Lyncestis** was built by Philip II of Macedonia. Excavations, begun in 1935, are still under way. Among the exciting discoveries are floor mosaics of gentle beauty and bronze statuettes. Back in modern Bitola, there are interesting mosques and churches, and the bazaar is as dynamic and colourful as a Macedonian folk dance.

sveti Naum. Or you can get there by boat, to feel the mood of Lake Ohrid with a view of Albania across the way. The monastery, on a bluff overlooking the lake, nudges against the frontier; you can see buoys demarcating the lake's nationality and, on a hill, the Albanian flag hoisted above the flat roof of an unlovely border post.

The Monastery of St. Naum was founded in the year 900 by

191

WHAT TO DO

Sports

From Alpine skiers to yachtsmen, sports lovers of almost every stripe give Yugoslavia high marks at any time of year. The busiest season is summer, obviously focusing on the advantages of the unpolluted Adriatic. Taking all the bays and peninsulas, inlets and islets into account, Yugoslavia's coastline totals some 6,000 beautiful kilometres (3,800 miles). This provides an infinity of escapist spots, yet in the most popular resorts at peak times the beaches do fill up. Relief is usually a short walk or boat ride away.

Whatever your sport, shun too much sun, particularly at midday. Red noses and blistering shoulders punish holiday-makers greedy for exposure. A cover-up is wiser, at least until your skin has become accustomed to the powerful rays. When the sun blazes, anoint yourself with a sun shield, wear a hat and shirt, or take cover under the beach umbrella.

Water Sports

The Adriatic, usually placid and extraordinarily transparent, couldn't be more inviting for **swimming.** The seashore consists of rocky coves, pebbly beaches, man-made embankments and sandy expanses. Depending on the locale, the facilities may range from little (perhaps an elementary shower) or nothing, to the sports equipment, parasols and attentive bar service available in the lee of luxury hotels.

Connoisseurs of sandy beaches find some of the well-known Yugoslavian resorts barely up to scratch: they have plenty of alluring seascapes, but shingle or pebble beaches instead of dreamy dunes. If you're manoeuvering barefoot on the rocks beware of jagged edges and stay clear of sea urchins; or pick up a pair of plastic sandals. In some resorts where there is sand, it's been imported, as, for instance, at Portorož and Opatija. On the plus side, there are naturally sandy beaches, for instance near Budva and Petrovac, and a seaside sahara beyond Ulcinj.

Inland, in idyllic settings, bathers enjoy Yugoslavia's famous lakes, such as Bled, Bohinj and Ohrid.

Snorkelling gives the swimmer an undistorted, uninterrupted view of the undersea world. Sporting-goods shops in the resort towns sell masks, breathing tubes and flippers, though you may find them expensive. Because

Running the rapids of the Sava Gorge, near the Austrian frontier.

of the Adriatic's renowned transparency and the proliferation of fish, these are appealing waters for the undersea fan.

Scuba diving is very tightly controlled. You need a permit from the local harbour authorities. Underwater fishing with scuba equipment is forbidden, as is retrieving archaeological relics. There are zones, such as shipping lanes or the area around ports or naval installations, where undersea activity is prohibited. In spite of all the red tape, the ideal visibility makes the effort worthwhile.

Boating. Yugoslavia has three dozen marinas. If you're visiting the country on your own boat, you must apply for a sailing permit at your first port of call. If you'd like to hire a yacht for a day or a week, this, too, can be arranged; a professional crew is optional. At certain beaches small sailing-boats can be hired; be sure to learn about the local winds before venturing too far. Rowing-boats and small motorboats are also available on an hourly basis. On the rivers canoes and kayaks provide exciting sport. And there are rafting excursions down the rapids, led by experts.

Water-skiing instruction and equipment are available at numerous resorts. **Para-skiing,** new to Yugoslavia, allows you to really take off.

Windsurfing (sailboarding) is gaining great popularity. At various sea and lake resorts you can hire equipment or sign up for lessons leading to a certificate. Instructors can even provide video critiques of a student's style.

Fishing in lakes and rivers and even the deep sea is enmeshed in regulations, affecting not only professionals but also the transient amateur angler. For the latest information on permits and limits, check with the local authorities when you reach your resort. Travel agencies on the spot sometimes organize fishing expeditions. Equipment may be bought in sporting-goods shops in the towns.

Sports Ashore

Interest in **tennis** is growing in Yugoslavia. Some resort hotels have their own courts; elsewhere look for a local tennis club.

Due in part to the mountainous terrain, the country's **golf** infrastructure is underdeveloped, making it very much a minority game. The best-known course, in lovely surroundings, is in Slovenia, on the outskirts of Bled. Elsewhere you may have to make do with **mini-golf,** a common enough diversion on the hotel circuit.

Horse riding is available, especially in Istria and the north, most famously at the Lipica stud. For youngsters there are establishments that have ponies for hire.

At Plava Laguna resort in Istria, riding is one of the optional extras.

Mountain-climbing. Challenging peaks rise all over Yugoslavia, from the northern frontier to southernmost Macedonia. The summit is Triglav, in the Julian Alps of Slovenia, which can be attacked from several directions. Several other mountains of interest to climbers and hikers are within striking distance of the Adriatic resorts. **Hang-gliding** is popular in mountainous parts.

Hunting for big and small game is a well-developed pursuit in the mountains and plains of Yugoslavia. At the big end of the scale, hunters look for brown bear, hart and wild boar. Elsewhere wild-fowl is the target. The big-game outings—package tours includ-ing accommodation, transport, a game licence and a guide—are very expensive. Specialist travel agencies and Yugoslavian tourist offices have details.

Skiing. World-class slopes and ever better facilities have made Yugoslavia a power to contend with in the winter sports market. Thanks to international televi-sion coverage of the big competi-tions, resorts like Krajnska Gora and Jahorina have become well known worldwide.

Yugoslavia's most sophisticat-ed ski station, Krajnska Gora, is so close to Austria and Italy that they sell three-nation ski passes. Nearby Planica is a renowned ski-jump centre, and the Bohinj and Bled areas offer good facil-ities and scenery. The only ski slopes within commuting dis-tance of the sea are at Platak and Delnice, above Rijeka; you could, theoretically, alternate be-tween skiing and swimming in April. In Serbia the big news is Kopaonik, a custom-built resort with all modern conveniences. Bosnia boasts Jahorina (near Sa-rajevo), which made its mark in the 1984 Winter Olympics. Mon-tenegro's budding winter resort, Žabljak, is surrounded by Durmi-tor National Park. Southernmost Macedonia, too, exploits its

snows, for instance at Popova Šapka, near Tetovo. Package-tour companies run ski holidays to the best-equipped ski spots.

Indoor Pursuits

Bowling alleys have been opened in some of the big tourist hotels along the coast. **Table tennis** is widely available. Scores of hotels have heated indoor **swimming** pools.

Chess is more of a major na-tional sport than in most Western countries. If you can play, it's a quick way to meet the Yugoslavs.

Spectator Sports

Football (soccer) is serious busi-ness throughout Yugoslavia, though the principal matches are held outside the tourist season. Still, you may stumble upon informal training sessions on one of the country's 4,500 football grounds.

Water polo. Each Adriatic vil-lage seems to field a team ready to drown for local honour. An excit-ing game to watch when spirits reach flood tide.

Watering Places

They've been doing it since the time of the ancient Romans: bathing in mineral-rich water hot from the spring, and drinking the stuff, hot or cold, in vast quanti-ties. Spa enthusiasts swear by it. And even if taking the waters doesn't cure your every ache and ailment, it's a relaxing, salubrious way to spend a week or two at any time of year.

As the Romans soon discovered, Yugoslavia is very well endowed in health-giving sources of water. They spring up all over the country, but the biggest concentration of spas is in the north. In some cases you can identify a spa by the name on the map or road sign; many of them have two-word names ending in *Toplice* or *Banja*, both of which mean "spa". (A cross-section of spas—Igalo, Ilidža, Opatija and Rogaška Slatina—is covered in the "Where to Go" section of this book.)

The modern Yugoslavian spas have medical personnel and all sorts of diagnostic and therapeutic facilities. But the creature comforts and recreational opportunities are worthy of holiday hotels.

Folklore and Entertainment

In most tourist spots, the best show in town is a rousing spectacle of local folklore, usually presented outdoors in the cool of the evening. The performers, likely to be semi-professionals or dedicated amateurs, demonstrate the songs and dances of the region, as well as the traditional entertainments of more remote Yugoslavian areas. The costumes, movements and music are exotic, colourful, perhaps incomprehensible... adding up to a memorable evening out.

The dances of Yugoslavia's regions are as varied as the people—you might as well compare a minuet and a belly dance. Some dances are prim and coy, others earthy, foot-stamping, whistling, shouting free-for-alls. As the regional spotlight shifts, the costumes and the pace change in a minute from the gaiety of a Slovenian polka, accordion music and all, to the frenzy of a Montenegrin sword dance.

Here's a cross-section of the song-and-dance spectacles you may experience in the tourist zones:

Istria. Accompanied by oboe and bagpipe, Istrian songs resemble the harsher, less melodious tunes of the Dinaric hinterland. But along the coast you'll probably hear Dalmatian folk songs, some rather Italian in character. The farther south you go the brighter the colours of the costumes.

Dalmatia. Guitars and mandolins provide the accompaniment for *klapa* songs, performed by a group of eight to 12 men singing softly. A typical dance of Dalmatia is the *lindjo*. Someone calls out the steps with humorous asides, as in American square dancing. Dangerous dancing is a feature of the island of Korčula, home of the *moreska* sword dance, derived from an ancient morality

197

play. The swords are real—sparks fly and performers have been known to be wounded.

Montenegro. Dancers link arms for the *kolo*, the basic circle dance, and there are sword dances, too. The "music" may be provided by stamping feet rather than instruments. The costumes are elaborate: luxurious, multi-layered extravaganzas in red, turquoise and pale blue. The men wear voluminous blue pantaloons tucked into high black-leather boots.

Inland, the Serbian *kolo* may be danced to bagpipe, flute, violin or accordion. Bosnia-Hercegovina's sometimes fierce dances eschew musical accompaniment. The Macedonian repertory includes both cheery and dreamy dances, and sword-swinging war dances *(rusali);* they have Greek, Turkish and Albanian overtones.

Festivals

Travelling through the Yugoslavian countryside you're likely to happen upon a village fair or saint's day or other religious or civic festivity. But you don't have to leave everything to chance. Ask at the local tourist office for the calendar of events in your area.

Attending a small-town fête is the most delightful way to absorb the flavour of Yugoslavia's authentic folklore. Perhaps the genuine traditions have been polished a bit to please the tourists, but you'll be swept up in the convivial, exciting fun.

Much bigger, and better organized, are these highlights among the country's annual events of international interest:

Belgrade. Spring festival of pop, folk and jazz music, May. Classical music festival, October.

Dubrovnik. Festival of drama, dance and music, July-August.

Ljubljana. Wedding festival, June.

Opatija. Opera, ballet and symphony festival, July-August.

Sarajevo. Yugoslavian song festival, April.

Skopje. Operatic evenings, May.

Split. Summer gala, July-August.

Zagreb. Folk festival, July.

Nightlife

The big resorts and busy inland cities offer a reasonably comprehensive range of nightlife possibilities. The sophistication of the entertainment may not be a

In sophisticated city of Ljubljana folk dancers and musicians can still draw a crowd.

match for Las Vegas or Monte Carlo, but there's no shortage of discos, nightclubs, even gambling casinos.

When it comes to cultural events—drama, concerts, opera and ballet—Belgrade and Zagreb can compete with cities of their size anywhere in Europe. And historic coastal towns like Dubrovnik, Pula, Split and Zadar stage plays and concerts in the setting of great monuments.

On a lighter note, live dance bands hold forth in the evenings at many of the large resort hotels, to which people gravitate from the less dynamic hotels. But you never know what you'll find along the coast; a fishing village could be hiding a raucous disco. In general, though, a night out in Yugoslavia winds up earlier than in, say, Spain or Italy.

Some of the big hotels round out the entertainment with gambling casinos where the chips are sold for foreign currency only. Roulette, chemin de fer, blackjack, craps and slot machines compete for your investment.

Or go to the cinema. Most of the films are foreign, shown with the original soundtrack and subtitles in one of the Yugoslavian languages. The quality of the offerings varies spectacularly, from fairly recent international hits to obscure examples of soft porn. In many places the films are shown outdoors in summer.

Shopping

The shopping scene in Yugoslavia is rich in promise and variety, even if a few white elephants show up among the works of art. Moreover, in the teeming market places you can still buy handicrafts from the artisans themselves, bypassing the middlemen and the markup. Acquiring typical trinkets from the locals can be a memorable experience of any holiday. But face-to-face transactions with the makers are becoming rarer; in most aspects of the souvenir business, mass production and distribution are now the norm.

Whether you choose to shop in

the open-air market or a department store or a small boutique, you probably won't go away empty-handed. The choice ranges from the perfectly portable (such as a pair of earrings) to the ponderous (how about an oriental carpet?).

Most of the prices are fixed, and haggling is a rarely played sport. But, if you enjoy bargaining, street pedlars and the owners of small handicraft shops may accept your challenge to negotiate the price.

When it comes to souvenirs, you'll enjoy browsing through a cross-section of regional crafts. And in the non-tourist shops you can see how and what the Yugoslavs buy. The food stores and supermarkets, too, provide an informal survey of the standard of living—and its cost.

Duty-free shops have become a commonplace in hotels all around the country. Anyone with foreign currency can buy a variety of goods at advantageous prices—anything from a carton

From biblical scenes to comic relief, a wood-carver in Rovinj keeps alive an old tradition.

of cigarettes to a hi-fi system or a nutria coat. Prices are normally listed in German marks; this keeps up with inflation and avoids quotations in millions of dinars, which might discourage potential buyers.

Shopping hours in the resorts follow the typical Mediterranean pattern—early morning to early evening with a long break during the heat of the afternoon. Typ-ically, shops stay open from 8 a.m. to noon, closing for lunch and a civilized siesta and reopening from 5 to 8 p.m. However, certain shops—especially supermarkets—do business all day without a break. These anti-siesta establishments are marked *nonstop*.

Many of the best souvenirs are typical of only one region or town; you may see them nowhere

else. But if you have the opportunity, compare prices from place to place. Generally the same item costs more in a resort than in an inland town.

Carpets lead Mostar shoppers into a labyrinth; in old Sarajevo an artisan embellishes a silver platter.

What to Buy

Here are a few ideas for the shopper, in alphabetical order. Well-travelled visitors consider these items either relatively cheap in Yugoslavia or unique—and sometimes both.

Carpets small enough for a doormat or big enough to cover your living room floor come in traditional or stylish modern designs. Original hand-loomed patterns meet high artistic standards, but even the machine-made patterns are distinctive.

Ceramics. For instance, hand-painted plates in bright colours and one-of-a-kind designs.

Copper coffee grinders, coffee pots and cups, platters, bracelets, all in the Turkish style, and usually inexpensive.

Crystal. Imaginatively designed and relatively inexpensive: glasses, candlesticks, bowls.

Embroidery ranges from handkerchiefs to lavishly decorated skirts and blouses giving a stylized impression of national costumes. At the markets it's usually the ladies who make them who sell them.

Filigree jewellery. This art flourishes in predominantly Muslim areas. Prices vary drastically from place to place.

Gramophone records and **tapes** are a bargain—folk music, the classics or a Balkan version of a pop song.

Knives for the kitchen, folding knives, even oriental-style daggers.

Lavender oil from Hvar is claimed to cure headaches, rheumatism, depression and other complaints, and it repels mosquitos.

Leather goods—belts, handbags, wallets, luggage, shoes—require a close look and some comparison shopping.

Musical instruments. A guitar, a flute or a single-stringed lute.

Postage stamps make cheap, thoughtful gifts for collectors on your list.

Ohrid "pearls" are manufactured by a secret process from the scales of a unique lake fish.

Naïve Art. Yugoslavian artists receive international attention for their unaffected paintings of bucolic scenes; but the prices can be shockingly sophisticated.

Reproductions of religious icons are amazingly authentic looking down to the last antique detail.

Spirits. Very inexpensive, often impressively packaged gifts, such as *maraskino* (morello-cherry flavour) and *šljivovica*, the plum brandy. But beware of shops selling spurious imported beverages, such as "original fine old *Skotch* malt whisky".

Wood carving. Salad sets, statuettes, egg cups, and knick-knacks mass-produced by hand. Also chess sets with fancifully carved armies of pieces.

EATING OUT

Yugoslavia's gastronomic traditions come from as far afield as the Austro-Hungarian and Ottoman empires. Goulash and strudel, baked lamb and sticky-sweet *baklava* are equally at home. And all the recipes, familiar or far-out, are enhanced by ingredients freshly harvested from farm, lake and sea.

Along the Adriatic, predictably, menus highlight seafood. But a change of pace is always at hand, for instance meat stews, stuffed cabbage, and charcoal-grilled *ćevapčići* sizzling with the spice of foreign intrigue. Generally speaking, Istrian and Dalmatian recipes follow Mediterranean traditions; in the northern plain the Hungarian influence is pronounced; and in Serbia and southern areas the trend is towards the piquant mystique of the orient.

To get the real taste of Yugoslavia you'll want to venture beyond the hotel dining room with its comfortable multilingual menus and what's likely to be bland "international" cuisine. In a "real" restaurant off the tourist track the menu *(jelovnik)* in Serbo-Croatian may baffle you. So be sure to take a look at our food list on page 237, or put yourself in the kindly hands of the waiter. He probably speaks German and a little English, or some eloquent sign language*.

In Yugoslavia the waiters take their jobs seriously, as indicated by the black bow ties and white shirts they wear, even in the simplest tavern. (The waitresses often sport prim hats and folkloric costumes, and always those orthopaedic-style, high white shoes with peekaboo heels and toes.) Incidentally, the waiter will come to take your drink order as soon as you sit down; the menu comes later. Not for the Yugoslavs the subtleties of matching wines and food.

Starters and Snacks

Pršut, smoked or air-dried ham, is cut paper-thin. Various regions have their own ways of preparing it, but the Dalmatian version, served along the coast, is famous for its subtle flavour.

Salama, in thin slices, is another popular starter. Usually a pork salami reminiscent of the Italian type, it can also be made of lamb, veal or poultry.

Kajmak, made with the skin of scalded milk, has a unique flavour and cheesy texture; usually to be spread on some bread or a roll.

---

* For a comprehensive glossary of Serbo-Croatian wining and dining terms ask your bookshop for the Berlitz EUROPEAN MENU READER. Restaurant hours are listed on page 236, along with a description of the types of establishment.

Cheese (*sir* in Serbo-Croatian) is often served as the first course. Each district produces its own, soft or hard, mild or sharp, depending on local taste. In Montenegro a slice of cheese is grilled (broiled) and served as a starter.

A savoury snack, often eaten at street stands, *burek* is a flaky pasty of cheese, minced meat, spinach, even apples.

If you're looking for a sandwich to bridge the gap until dinnertime, you may be offered a pair of extra-thick slices of dry bread enclosing a minimal slice of cheese, ham or bologna.

Soups

Categorized either as *supa*, a broth, or *čorba* (a thick soup), they come in many varieties and may be grouped together as *juha*. Even the clear soups—chicken and beef broth lengthily simmered with vegetables and noodles—tend to be wholesome and filling.

Brodet is a seafood stew enlivened by herbs and white wine, calling to mind the *bouillabaisse* of the French Riviera.

Pasulj, Serbian bean soup, is a hearty hotpot of white beans, smoked pork and peppers.

Gulaš soup, a Hungarian invention, is known and loved as a local speciality in various regions of Yugoslavia. This spicy beef-based soup comes as thick as a stew.

Fish and Shellfish

Along the coast, *jastog*, lobster, takes star billing (as the whopping bill will indicate). It's usually boiled, then served cold with mayonnaise. Other seafood possibilities include squid, crab, scampi and oysters.

Along the Adriatic, outdoor dining features the local seafood and wine.

206

In many restaurants you'll be invited to choose your fish from the refrigerated display case. At the seaside the usual method of preparing mackerel *(skuše),* red mullet *(barbun),* bass *(brancin)* or similar-sized fish is grilling over charcoal, with a strong hint of garlic.

Inland, fish is more often boiled or fried. The freshwater range includes *jesetra* (sturgeon), *pastrmka* (trout) and *šaran* (carp). A very special delicacy, salmon trout from Lake Ohrid, has pink flesh as meaty as a sea fish. There are two varieties: *letnica* and *belvica.*

Meat Dishes

Ćevapčići, perhaps the most ubiquitous of all Yugoslavian dishes, are small sausage-shaped patties of minced meat, charcoal grilled

Bread in Novi Pazar means Turkish-style pide.

and served with chopped raw onion. Depending on the region, the main ingredient may be mutton, pork or beef. Ten is the usual portion.

Ražnjići: the same idea but featuring large skewered chunks of pork or veal; two skewers is the standard quantity.

As if to prove that there's more to Yugoslavian cooking than kebabs, the Serbs invented *djuveč*, a casserole of lamb or pork with rice, peppers, aubergine (eggplant), carrots, beans, potatoes, onions, cheese and whatever else captures the chef's imagination.

Sogan dolma, stuffed courgettes (zucchini) enhanced by a tasty cream sauce, is a rich Bosnian preparation.

Musaka, familiar all over the Middle East as well as Yugoslavia, consists of layers of minced meat alternating with potato, aubergine or courgettes, ovenbrowned.

Fowl and Game

Piletina (chicken) and *ćuretina* (turkey) are commonly served roasted or in stews. During the hunting season you may want to try a more elusive bird such as *jarebica* (partridge) or *fazan*

pickled vegetables like cucumber, cabbage, peppers and tomatoes.

Boiled vegetables and boiled, fried or roast potatoes are the most common accompaniments.

Desserts

The pastries here show two rich influences, Turkish and Viennese. So if it isn't sugar, nuts and poppyseeds, it has to be whipped cream.

People with a sweet tooth rave about the *baklava*, flaky pastry enriched with walnuts, eggs and butter and steeped in syrup. Another remnant of Turkish times is *lokum*, known elsewhere as Turkish delight.

Palačinke—pancakes filled with chopped nuts and adorned with jam or chocolate sauce or ice-cream—may be a vestige of Austro-Hungary. But they are available in many parts of Yugoslavia having no imperial connections. Even humble pizzerias know how to make them.

You'll think you're in Budapest or Vienna when you taste the strudel *(štrudla)*, airy pastry filled with apples or cherries, cheese or poppyseeds. A sophisticated variation: *zagorski štruklji*, sugared pastry with a cottage cheese and egg filling.

Or try a fruit salad *(voćna salata)*. In some other countries, curiously, this is known as a *macédoine*, honouring, for hazy reasons, Macedonia.

(pheasant). In Istria, under the Italian influence, they do an appealing chicken risotto served with grated cheese. (This is one of the few Istrian dishes not accompanied by polenta, the staple maize-meal pudding.)

Salads and Vegetables

In both simple and elegant restaurants salads often accompany the main dish. A favourite is *Srpska salata* (Serbian salad), a refreshing plate of tomatoes and onion. Otherwise, any of the fresh vegetables appearing in the market may turn up on the salad plate, such as radish, peppers, cucumber and dandelion. And out of season they make salads of

Yugoslavia's Wines

From earthy reds to refreshing rosés to delicate whites, Yugoslavia's wines complement every kind of dish. You will be doubly delighted to discover that many of the local wines are first-class but priced beneath their dignity.

Wine has been made and enjoyed in Yugoslavia since the time of the ancient Greeks. International experts give the modern vintages good reviews. But you don't have to be a connoisseur to appreciate them. Start at the grass roots, or the vines, wherever you are and order a carafe of the house wine. All you need to know at this stage is the colour: *Bjelo* is white, *ružica*, rosé, and *crno* (literally black) means red wine. Mineral water is often served as well; diluting wine in the glass is an optional custom.

There are vineyards in practically all parts of Yugoslavia except the least inviting mountains. Here's a selection of some of the more interesting of them:

Blatina: a virile red wine from Mostar.

Dingač: a full-bodied red from Dalmatia's Pelješac peninsula.

Grk: no vowels but plenty of punch in this exceedingly dry white wine from the island of Korčula.

Kutjevo: varied wines of high standard from northern Croatia.

Malvazija: a smooth but strong white variety from Istria.

Merlot: also Istrian, a ruby-coloured red wine.

Prošek: a tawny-coloured, strong dessert wine from the Dalmatian coast.

Ljutomer rizling: a fine white wine from Slovenia.

Žilavka: a delicate, fruity white from Hercegovina.

Other Beverages

On a hot summer day you may choose to abandon wine in favour of a cool beer. Yugoslavian lagers are normally sold only in large bottles. They're much cheaper than imported brands, which come in small bottles.

Fruit juices—everything from apricot and blueberry to peach and strawberry—are cheap and wholesome. Local imitations of foreign soft drinks are less successful; name brands, bottled locally under license, cost more than some wines.

The wide range of mineral waters includes healthful-tasting *Radenska,* thirst-quenching *Jamnička* and *Knjaz Miloš* from Bokovićka Banja, whose label still advertises that it won a Grand Prix at Brussels in 1906. Some restaurants simply serve mineral water *(mineralne vode)* anonymously in carafes, bubbly *(gazarine)* unless you specify otherwise *(negazarine).*

Espresso coffee *(espreso kafu)* is dispensed along the coast and less commonly as an option inland, where tiny cups of thick, syrupy Turkish coffee *(turska kava)* are an important part of local life. Some cafés also serve *cappuccino* and *eis kafe* (iced coffee with ice-cream and whipped cream). Tea drinkers have reported some disappointments with the local brew.

Spirits
Rakija is the generic term embracing all the various fruit brandies you're likely to come across. They are cheap and powerful. The locals are liable to down one before dinner as well as after.

Many hotel bars serve pre-dinner cocktails, more popular with tourists than with Yugoslavs. A local aperitif, milder than most, is *Istra Bitter*, a herb tonic. Imported brands of aperitifs and other spirits are expensive.

Šljivovica, distilled from plums, is the most famous and popular Yugoslavian fruit brandy. It may pack more of a punch than you expect. Or try one of the alternative firewaters, *lozovača* (grape brandy) or *kajsijevača* (apricot brandy). And don't overlook *maraskino*, the spirit made from morello cherries.

Finally, *vinjak* is a local brandy reminiscent of French cognac at less than half the price.

BERLITZ-INFO

CONTENTS

Listed after each main entry is its appropriate Serbo-Croatian translation, usually in the singular. You'll find this vocabulary useful when asking for assistance. Because of the linguistic variations you may encounter in different regions, an alternative translation is sometimes indicated in brackets []. If the first expression brings a blank look, try the second.

A ACCOMMODATION

See also CAMPING. Depending on budget and taste, visitors to Yugoslavia can choose to stay at international-class luxury hotels— or opt for the cosy simplicity of a room in a private house. For stays in resort areas during July and August, it's wise to make reservations well in advance; in towns and cities elsewhere in the country, bookings are recommended all year round. If you arrive on short notice without a reservation, the local tourist office usually can solve the problem on the spot. But you may have to settle for an unexpectedly modest roof over your head.

Hotels *(hotel)* in Yugoslavia are officially graded in five categories. "L" is de luxe and from there the ratings descend from A to D, which is the lowest grade to earn the title of hotel. The classifications are designed to give you an idea of what facilities are offered and what they might cost. Hotels set their own rates, normally linked to U.S. dollars or German marks as a defence against inflation. Prices vary according to certain factors, including the popularity of the resort. Breakfast is usually included in the price. For stays of more than three days, hotels provide accommodation and three meals a day for an advantageous fixed price. Out of season, hotels in resort areas, including the relatively few de luxe establishments, offer big reductions. A complete list of hotels with their facilities and seasonal rates is available from Yugoslav tourist offices. A visitors' tax is levied regardless of the kind of accommodation involved; it varies from resort to resort. The tax is normally halved in the off-season.

A note about passports: when you arrive at your hotel, the receptionist will take your passport so it can be registered. It is routinely returned the next morning. In the meantime, there is no cause for concern: the passport, and you, are perfectly safe.

Motels *(motel)* are situated along a main highway or on the edge of town. Most offer facilities similar to a B-class hotel. Car-repair services and fuel may be available.

Boarding houses *(pansion)*. Comfortable, but with fewer facilities than a hotel. Officially these establishments are graded in three categories, I to III.

Tourist Villages *(turističko naselje)*. A self-contained resort. May consist of bungalows or low-rise hotel facilities built around a central core of restaurants, shops and public rooms.

Apartments and Villas *(stan; vila)*. Popular with tourists who prefer a self-catering holiday, but it may be difficult to make arrangements on short notice. Write to inquire at the tourist office in the resort of your choice.

Rooms *(Soba)*. In some of the popular resorts, rooms for tourists in private homes outnumber hotel rooms. They're closely supervised and graded (from I to III) according to the degree of comfort provided. Accommodation, sometimes including meals, can be arranged through the local tourist office. Landladies canvassing near ferry and bus terminals sometimes descend on arriving tourists.

Youth and student hostels *(omkadinski dom; studentski dom)*. You can obtain a list of Yugoslav hostels and their facilities from your own national youth-hostels association. There's no age limit, but priority is given to visitors under 27.

An organization specializing in holidays and travel for young people and students, *Karavan-Naromtravel*, runs youth centres in Dubrovnik, Rovinj, Bečići and Kopaonik. For information and bookings apply to the organization's headquarters at Knez Mihailova 50, 11000 Belgrade, tel. 187-822.

Young tourists can also live economically at university halls of residence.

a double/single room	**soba sa dva kreveta/sa jednim krevetom**
with/without bath	**sa kupatilom/bez kupatila**
What's the rate per night?	**Koliko košta za jednu noć?**

AIRPORTS *(aerodrom)*

Numerous Yugoslavian airports, from Ljubljana in the north to Ohrid in the south, are open to international traffic. The principal international lines serve Belgrade and Zagreb. Most of the tourist flights concentrate on the key coastal airports, serving Pula, Rijeka, Split and Dubrovnik. All the busy airports are equipped with restaurants or snack bars, car-hire agencies, duty-free shops and taxi ranks. Currency-exchange offices operate in the arrival areas, but there is no way departing passengers can change their dinars back into foreign currencies. Charter flights are met by tourist-agency buses. Alternatively airline or local buses take passengers from the airports to town.

The recommended check-in time for departure generally is two hours before flight time for international destinations and one hour on domestic flights. Confirm the times with the airline or your tour-agency representative. And save some dinars for the departure tax, payable at the check-in counter.

Pula Airport, only 6 kilometres (4 mi.) from town, is the closest to a resort. Charters and seasonal lines make up most of the traffic.

Rijeka Airport is actually on the northern tip of the island of Krk, linked to the mainland by a bridge.

Kaštel Štafilić, the principal airport serving the central Dalmatian coast, lies just off the Adriatic Highway 25 kilometres (16 mi.) north of **Split.**

Passengers bound for **Dubrovnik** and the southern coast normally use the modern international airport at Ćilipi, 24 kilometres (15 mi.) south-east of Dubrovnik.

Porter!	Nosač!
Taxi!	Taksi!
Where's the bus for...?	Gde je autobus za...?

C CAMPING (kampovanje)

Yugoslavia has plenty of facilities for campers, particularly along the Adriatic coast and its islands. Many sites occupy privileged situations of natural beauty. In addition to electrical and sanitary installations and shops, amenities may include restaurants, garages and entertainment. Some sites also have bungalows and chalets. Rates depend on the setting and the extent of services provided. Like boarding houses, campsites are rated class I, II or III.

Camping is permitted only at official sites. Elsewhere, permission must be obtained from the local authorities. Simply pulling up for the night at the side of the road is quite illegal.

A free booklet listing campsites throughout Yugoslavia, complete with charts of facilities and prices, is published each year by the Automobile Association of Yugoslavia (AMSJ). The booklet is available at tourist offices or direct from AMSJ (address: Ruzveltova 18, 11000 Beograd, Yugoslavia.)

Is there a campsite near here?	**Da li ima kamp u blizini?**
May we camp here?	**Možemo li ovde kampovati?**
We have a tent/caravan.	**Imamo šator/prikolicu.**
What's the charge...?	**Koliko košta...?**
per person/for a car	**po osobi/za kola**
for a tent/for a caravan (trailer)	**za šator/za prikolicu**

CAR HIRE *(rent a kar)*

See also DRIVING. Half a dozen car-rental firms operate agencies in resorts large and small, as well as in the inland towns. If you haven't reserved a car before leaving home, you may well be able to organize things with the help of your hotel.

There are innumerable variants in price depending on the firm involved, the model of car, the length of time you use it and whether you plan to return it to the same place or elsewhere inside Yugoslavia or abroad. Chauffered cars may also be arranged.

A local tax may be included in the rate; non-deductible collision insurance is always added to the bill.

You must, of course, have a valid driving licence, held for at least one or two years; the minimum age is generally 21. Unless you pay by credit card, you'll be required to leave a refundable deposit. Depending on which credit card you use, some agencies may offer a discount of 10 to 20%.

Hiring a car for a day usually means from 8 a.m. to 8 p.m.

I'd like to rent a car.	**Hteo bih da rentiram kola.**
for one day/a week	**za jedan dan/jednu nedelju**
Please include full insurance.	**Sa potpunim osiguranjem molim Vas.**

CIGARETTES, CIGARS, TOBACCO *(cigarete, cigare, duvan)*

Yugoslavian cigarettes come in a strong, black Turkish variety, as well as in milder, western-European type blends. In addition, certain American brands are manufactured in Yugoslavia under licence. In larger towns and resorts a few British brands may also be found. The local cigarettes cost only a fraction of the retail price of the imports.

Tobacco shops also sell imported (usually Cuban) cigars and Yugoslavian pipe tobacco, which is highly regarded by connoisseurs.

Smoking is forbidden in cinemas, shops and on public transport; the Yugoslavian airline, JAT, prohibits smoking on domestic flights.

A packet of cigarettes/ *matches.*	**Kutiju cigareta/šibica.**
filter-tipped	**sa filterom**
without filter	**bez filtera**
light tobacco	**blagi duvan**
dark tobacco	**ljuti duvan**

CLIMATE

The sunniest part of Yugoslavia is the Adriatic coast, with its Mediterranean climate. The island of Hvar, south of Split, basks in an average of 2,725 sunny hours per year, more than some of the better publicized western-European sunspots. Winter on the coast is short and not too chilly, except when the dreaded *bura* wind roars in from the north. Spring comes early: the fruit trees and flowers bloom in March. Summer days are hot but the nights refresh. Autumn is usually warm and pleasant. However, drenching rainy spells can occur just about any time. Sea bathing can usually be enjoyed from spring to late autumn along much of the coast.

Inland Yugoslavia has a continental climate featuring hot summers and cold winters. The mountains are covered with ski-worthy snow from December until the end of March.

Monthly average maximum and minimum daytime temperatures* in degrees Fahrenheit:

		J	F	M	A	M	J	J	A	S	O	N	D
Belgrade	max.	37	42	52	64	73	79	83	83	76	64	51	42
	min.	26	29	36	45	54	59	62	62	56	47	39	32
Dubrovnik	max.	53	55	58	63	70	78	83	82	77	69	62	56
	min.	42	43	47	52	58	65	69	69	64	57	51	46

And in degrees Celsius:

		J	F	M	A	M	J	J	A	S	O	N	D
Belgrade	max.	3	5	11	18	23	26	28	28	24	18	11	5
	min.	-3	-2	2	7	12	15	17	17	13	8	4	0
Dubrovnik	max.	12	13	14	17	21	25	29	28	25	21	17	14
	min.	6	6	8	11	14	18	21	21	18	14	10	8

* Minimum temperatures are measured just before sunrise, maximum temperatures in the afternoon.

CLOTHING

The Adriatic coast demands lightweight clothing from June to September—the lighter the better. But on the fringes of the high season—before July and after the end of September—you may well need a jacket or sweater in the evening. Winter is the rainy season, but you might find a raincoat handy at any time of year.

Inland, you'll need cool cottons in the summer and a warm coat, hat and boots to fend off the winter chill.

Formality in dress is confined to sophisticated night-clubs and casinos. Elsewhere it's all very egalitarian. Rare is the restaurant where anyone is fussy about what clothes are worn, even though the waiters may dress ever so formally. On the beaches there is no prudery. However, it's reasonable to slip something over your bathing suit for the walk to and from the beach.

Obviously, when visiting churches or mosques modest dress is appropriate. And don't forget to wear comfortable shoes when you visit museums or go sightseeing. Just take them off before you enter a mosque.

COMMUNICATIONS

Post office *(pošta)*. Airmail is recommended for all destinations unless time is irrelevant. Registered letters and parcels must be presented unsealed; the postal clerk will seal them in your presence. You can also buy stamps where postcards are sold, for instance at newsstands and tobacconists.

Letter boxes in Yugoslavia, square and painted yellow, are normally affixed to walls. Post offices are marked by yellow PTT signs.

Poste restante (general delivery). If you don't know ahead of time where you'll be staying, you can have mail addressed to you in any town you'll be visiting, in care of the local post office—*post restant*, as the service is called in Yugoslavia. You'll have to show your passport and pay a small fee to retrieve your mail.

Telegrams *(telegram)*. All post offices accept telegrams. In the bigger towns the telegraph window at the main post office is open 24 hours a day. Some post offices also handle **telex** messages; or try your hotel desk.

Telephone *(telefon)*. Most public places have coin-operated telephones for local calls. An increasing number of pay phones can be used for long-distance, too, but you need a lot of coins. For calls abroad its best to go to the local post office. In most localities in

Yugoslavia you can dial direct to western Europe. Or, if you prefer, your hotel switchboard should be able to place any calls, local or international. A service charge may be added.

express (special delivery)	**ekspres**
airmail	**avionom**
registered	**preporučeno**
A stamp for this letter/ postcard, please.	**Molim Vas marku za ovo pismo/ za ovu kartu.**
May I use your telephone?	**Mogu li se poslužiti Vašim telefo- nom?**

COMPLAINTS

Complaint procedures vary according to the situation.

Hotels and restaurants. See the manager if you're dissatisfied. If this leads nowhere, the local tourist office may be able to help.

Bad merchandise. The consumer-oriented society is too new in Yugoslavia to have devised elaborate safeguards. Your best bet is to return to the shop and appeal to the manager's sense of fair play.

Car repairs. If your car has been badly repaired, or if you believe you have been overcharged, try to settle the problem before paying the bill. If this fails, the local tourist bureau may be able to suggest further steps.

Other services (shoe repairs and the like). By law, prices should be posted, but to avoid misunderstanding, it's wise to ask the cost in advance.

You can always lodge a complaint with Yugoslavia's Board of Trade Inspectors *(Tržišna inspekcija)*. Officials are polite and helpful, but it does take time for them to carry out their investigations. You may have left the country before a complaint can be verified.

CRIME AND THEFT

Violent crime is rare in Yugoslavia, but pickpockets and sneak thieves know no frontiers. In resort areas thefts pick up in the tourist season, so it's prudent to store valuables in the safe deposit box in your hotel. Lock your car and, if you're camping, close your tent well.

If you need to report a crime and there's no policeman in sight, the nearest tourist office or hotel should be able to put you in quick touch with the *milicija* (police).

I want to report a theft.	**Želim da prijavim kradju.**
My... has been stolen.	**Meni su ukrali...**
handbag	**tašnu**
passport	**pasoš**
wallet	**novčanik [lisnicu]**

CUSTOMS AND ENTRY REGULATIONS

To enter Yugoslavia all travellers must present a valid passport. Citizens of Great Britain and Ireland need no visas. American and Canadian citizens are automatically given entry visas upon arrival. No health certificate is required. If in doubt about visa formalities, check with your travel agent before you leave home. You're generally entitled to stay in Yugoslavia up to 90 days.

Here's what you can bring into Yugoslavia duty-free:

	Cigarettes		Cigars		Tobacco	Liquor	Wine
Yugoslavia	200	or	50	or	250 g.	1 l.	
Australia	200	or	250	or	250 g.	1 l. or 1 l.	
Canada	200	and	50	and	900 g.	1.1 l. or 1.1 l.	
Eire	200	or	50	or	250 g.	1 l. and 2 l.	
N. Zealand	200	or	50	or	250 g.	1.1 l. and 4.5 l.	
S. Africa	400	and	50	and	250 g.	1 l. and 2 l.	
U.K.	200	or	50	or	250 g.	1 l. and 2 l.	
U.S.A.	200	and	100	and	*	1 l. and 1 l.	
* A reasonable quantity							

In addition to personal clothing and jewellery, you are allowed a small amount of perfume and ¼ litre of cologne. Note that visitors are required to declare cameras, cassette recorders, video apparatus and the like on arrival. The number and type of articles will be entered in your passport, and cancelled when you leave.

Before your trip, ask for the customs notice listing duty-free allowances for your own country.

Currency restrictions. While you may bring unlimited sums of foreign currency into Yugoslavia, you may not carry more than

50,000 dinars (in denominations no larger than 5,000 dinars) across the border in either direction. And this amount can only be imported or exported once per calendar year. On subsequent trips, the quota is 20,000 dinars.

I have nothing to declare.	**Nemam ništa za carinjenje.**
It's for my personal use.	**To je za moju ličnu upotrebu.**

D DRIVING

To take your car to Yugoslavia you will need:

- A valid driving licence; an International Driving Permit is recommended but not required
- Car registration papers
- Green Card (international insurance certificate)
- Nationality plate or sticker visible at rear of the car
- First-aid kit
- Red warning triangle for display in case of breakdown
- A set of spare bulbs

Drivers and passengers of cars fitted with seat belts are required to wear them.

Motorcycle or scooter drivers, as well as passengers, must wear helmets.

Driving regulations. As elsewhere on the Continent, drive on the right, overtake (pass) on the left. At intersections, yield right of way to vehicles coming from the right unless otherwise indicated.

Speed limits. 60 kilometres per hour (kph) in towns, 80 kph outside built-up areas, 100 kph on main roads, 120 kph on motorways (highways). In practice, Yugoslav drivers interpret speed regulations most flexibly.

Road conditions. The main roads are generally good, but secondary roads are unpredictable; a smooth surface can deteriorate to a collection of bone-jarring potholes in the blink of an eye, sometimes without warning. In addition, unforeseen obstructions, such as pedestrians or livestock, may catch you off-guard. On mountain roads, rockfalls are a daily event; along main routes, workmen are out at dawn to sweep up, but on back roads you must be ready for anything. Drive with special care and patience in villages, where people traditionally stroll in the middle of the road, day and night. Yugoslavia's scanty motorway mileage is expanding. But note that some toll roads are simply well-paved two-lane thoroughfares with fewer crossroads (intersections) than ordinary roads.

Parking. In larger towns parking meters are abundant; economy-minded local drivers often gamble that the police are too busy to check them. Car parks have also been introduced, sometimes complete with parking meters. In many towns parking is an unstructured, pragmatic affair, with drivers taking over the edges of parks and squares and almost any open place not specifically forbidden.

Incidentally, wherever you park—on city streets or country roads—the law requires that you stop in the direction of moving traffic, on the right-hand side. And if you leave your car in a no-parking zone it may be towed away.

Breakdowns. The Automobile Association of Yugoslavia (AMSJ) runs a comprehensive network of aid and information offices. They're open from 8 a.m. to 8 p.m. You can call on them for help in most places by dialling 987. Towing equipment and mechanics are stationed at more than 170 bases around the country.

Garages specializing in the repair of leading makes of car are found only in the larger cities. Elsewhere, privately run garages can probably tide you over with ingenious stop-gap methods. But insist on a realistic price estimate in advance. Spare parts are readily available for cars assembled in Yugoslavia: Citroën, Fiat, Renault, Volkswagen and Yugo. For other cars replacement parts might be very difficult to come by, but the automobile association can help expedite urgent shipments.

Fuel and oil. Filling stations are well distributed around the country, particularly in towns and along major roads. Many provide 24-hour service. The grades of fuel available are normal (86 octane), super (98 octane), unleaded (still uncommon) and diesel.

Petrol coupons. These coupons, which make possible a slight reduction in fuel costs, can be bought at travel agencies, at automobile clubs in the country of departure and at the Yugoslavian frontier. Unused coupons can be refunded at the border when leaving the country or at the place where they were purchased. Ask your automobile club about the latest regulations.

Note that it is forbidden to enter Yugoslavia with a spare supply of petrol in the car.

Fluid measures

imp.gals.0   5   10

litres 0   5   10   20   30   40   50

U.S.gals.0   5   10

Distance

Kilometres to miles

km	0	1	2	3	4	5	6		8		10		12		14		16
miles	0	½	1	1½	2		3		4		5		6		7		8		9		10

Road signs. The standard international pictographs are used in Yugoslavia. You'll also encounter the following written notices:

Centar grada	Town centre
Crna tačka	Black spot (Danger)
Garaža	Garage
Milicija	Police
Odron kamenja	Falling rocks
Opasna krivina	Dangerous curve
Opasnost	Danger
Pozor	Attention
Radovi na putu	Road works (Men working)
Stoj	Stop
Škola	School
Uspon	Steep hill
driving licence	**vozačka dozvola**
car registration papers	**saobraćajna dozvola**
Green Card	**zelena karta**
Are we on the right road for...?	**Da li je ovo put za...?**
Full tank, please.	**Napunite, molim Vas.**
Check the oil/tires/battery.	**Proverite ulje/gume/akumulator.**
I've had a breakdown.	**Kola su mi u kvaru.**
There's been an accident/ a serious accident.	**Dogodila se saobraćajna nezgoda/nesreća.**

E **ELECTRIC CURRENT** *(električna struja)*
The standard voltage throughout Yugoslavia is 220 volt, 50-cycle A.C. Note that transformers and plug adaptors for American appliances cannot be purchased in Yugoslavia.

224

If your hair-dryer or other electrical appliance should break down, ask your hotel desk-clerk if he can recommend an electrical repair shop or local handyman.

I'd like an adaptor/a battery.	**Želim adaptor/bateriju.**

EMBASSIES AND CONSULATES *(ambasada; konzulat)*
All embassies are in Belgrade. Some countries maintain consulates in other cities as well.

Canada *Embassy:* Kneza Miloša 75, Belgrade; tel. 644-666

Great Britain *Embassy:* Generala Ždanova 46, Belgrade; tel. 645-055
Consulate: Ilica 12, Zagreb; tel. 424-888
Titova obala 10, Split; tel. 41-464

U.S.A. *Embassy:* Kneza Miloša 50, Belgrade; tel. 645-655
Consulate General: Braće Kavurića 2, Zagreb; tel. 444-800

Where's the British/American Embassy?	**Gde je Britanska/Američka ambasada?**
It's very urgent.	**Veoma je hitno.**

EMERGENCIES
In most cities the standard number to telephone in an emergency is 94. Note that you need a coin to dial this or any other number from a pay phone.

Depending on the nature of the emergency, refer to the separate entries in this section, such as EMBASSIES, HEALTH AND MEDICAL CARE and POLICE. Or put your problem in the hands of your hotel desk-clerk or travel-agency representative, or a taxi driver.

Though we hope you'll never need them, here are a few key words you might like to learn:

Careful	**Oprezno**
Fire	**Vatra**
Help	**U pomoć**
Police	**Milicija**
Stop	**Stanite**
Stop thief	**Držite lopova**

As fares and routes are constantly changing, it's best to consult a dependable, well-informed travel agent for up-to-date information. The following outline suggests some of the varied possibilities.

By Air

Scheduled flights. Direct flights link British centres with Yugoslavia's Adriatic airports—Pula, Rijeka, Split and Dubrovnik. There are also connections to the holiday areas via Zagreb. Extra flights are added during the peak tourist period.

Travellers heading for inland areas of Yugoslavia have the choice of direct flights to Belgrade, Zagreb and Ljubljana from London, Manchester and Glasgow.

Belgrade, Zagreb and Ljubljana are on the transatlantic time-tables, with direct flights from gateways as diverse as New York, Los Angeles, Cleveland, Chicago, Toronto and Montreal. All the regional airports, including the Adriatic resort destinations, are linked to the big cities by domestic JAT routes.

Charter flights and package tours. Various tour operators in the U.K. and Eire offer package holidays in all price ranges to Yugoslavian resorts.

The all-in package tour—flight, hotel and board included—remains a popular way of visiting the coast. Most tour agents recommend cancellation insurance, a modestly-priced safeguard: you lose no money if illness or accident forces you to cancel your holiday.

North American packages featuring the Adriatic resorts include air fare, transfers, accommodation, sightseeing, and some or all meals. Some tours combine the highlights of Yugoslavia with forays into neighbouring countries such as Italy, Austria, Hungary, Bulgaria, Romania or Greece.

By Car

Whether you drive through Germany and Austria or through France and Italy, you'll be able to travel on motorways (expressways) most of the way (paying tolls in France and Italy). Alternatively you can put your car on a train in northern Europe (May to September only). The car-sleeper express, while expensive, saves on fuel, wear and tear and hotel bills. You take the wheel again at Ljubljana or Rijeka. Yet another way to avoid many hours on the road: drive through Italy and take a car ferry across the Adriatic. Among many ferry options: Venice–Dubrovnik, Ancona–Zadar, Pescara–Split, and Bari–Bar.

By Rail

From London via Paris, the Simplon Express serves Ljubljana, Zagreb and Belgrade. Other good trains link the main Yugoslavian cities with Ostend, Venice, Munich and Vienna.

The Inter-Rail Card and Rail-Europ S (senior) ticket are valid in Yugoslavia, but the Eurailpass is not accepted.

GUIDES AND INTERPRETERS *(vodič; tumač)*

Most tourists need no special assistance; hotel personnel can deal with routine linguistic problems, and the travel agencies provide competent multi-lingual guides to conduct their tours. Businessmen or other visitors in search of translators or interpreters should inquire at the local tourist bureau.

We'd like an English-speaking guide.	**Hteli bismo engleskog vodiča.**
I need an English interpreter.	**Treba mi prevodilac za engleski jezik.**

HAIRDRESSERS *(frizer)*   **H**

Modern hairdressing establishments and old-fashioned barber shops are abundant everywhere in Yugoslavia. Prices are more than double at salons in the luxury hotels, compared with the neighbourhood shops. Tip about 10%.

haircut	**šišanje**
shave	**brijanje**
shampoo and set	**pranje kose i češljanje**
permanent wave	**trajna ondulacija**
colour chart	**pregled boja**
colour rinse	**preliv**
manicure	**manikir**
Don't cut it too short.	**Nejmojte suviše kratko.**
A little more off (here).	**Odrežite još malo (ovde).**
How much do I owe you?	**Koliko sam dužan?**

HEALTH AND MEDICAL CARE

Most tourists who suffer health problems in Yugoslavia have only themselves to blame—for overdoing the sunbathing or nightlife. If you want to protect a delicate stomach, be wary of adventurous foods for the first few days and stick to the excellent mineral waters.

Citizens of half a dozen western European countries, including Great Britain, are entitled to free medical care under reciprocal agreements with Yugoslavia. Citizens of other countries must pay for medical services. The charges are low by most standards, but be sure your health insurance covers illness or accident abroad.

For help in minor emergencies look for an *apoteka* or *ljekarna* (chemists or pharmacy) or an *ambulanta* (first-aid post) displaying a red cross.

Chemists (pharmacies). An *apoteka* supplies over-the-counter non-prescription remedies as well as medicines made up according to a prescription. A *drogerija* sells a great range of toilet articles, cosmetics, and sometimes films.

In the window of an *apoteka* you'll see a notice giving the address of the nearest all-night establishment. In large towns, some chemists are routinely open day and night. They are listed in the local newspaper.

If you're required to take certain medications regularly, bring an adequate supply from home. Specific brands of medicine might not be available locally in Yugoslavia, and dosages can be different.

a doctor	**doktor [lekar]**
an ambulance	**kola za hitnu pomoć**
hospital	**bolnica**
an upset stomach	**pokvaren stomak**
sunstroke	**sunčanica**
a fever	**groznica**

HITCH-HIKING *(autostop)*

Hitch-hiking is permitted but not necessarily gratifying, in spite of the general generosity of Yugoslavian drivers. On back roads the traffic can be very sparse, and in any event most of the passing cars tend to be loaded with passengers and cargo.

Can you give us a lift to...?	**Možete li nas povesti do...?**

HOURS

Banks generally open for business between 8 a.m. and 7 p.m. Monday to Friday, and from 8 a.m. to noon on Saturdays. Branches outside the big cities generally close for a lunch break.

Consulates/Embassies are usually open Monday to Friday from 8 or 8.30 a.m. to 12.30 or 1 p.m. and again in the afternoon on certain days.

Offices. 7 or 7.30 a.m. to 3 or 3.30 p.m. Monday to Friday.

Shops. In major cities and resorts, most self-service shops, department stores and food shops do business nonstop from 8 a.m. to 8 p.m. Monday to Friday and again Saturday morning. But many smaller establishments honour the siesta, closing between noon and 4 or 5 p.m. Some shops open Sunday morning as well.

Post offices. 8 a.m. to 8 p.m. in cities and big resorts, but in small towns a four-hour midday break interrupts the postal day.

Museums. Hours vary but the best bet is between 9 a.m. and 1 p.m. Tuesday to Sunday. The closing day is usually Monday.

LANGUAGE   L

In this Balkan Babel three major languages are spoken, plus an assortment of minor languages. Complicating matters, two alphabets are in use. The Latin alphabet, to which we're accustomed, is found in Slovenia and Croatia, as well as in parts of Bosnia-Hercegovina; elsewhere a form of the Cyrillic alphabet, common to the Slavic languages, is used.

The majority language, Serbo-Croatian, is understood in all parts of the country. Slovenian is spoken in the north-west and Macedonian in the south-east. Fortunately, these three Slavic languages have many similarities. Other languages—Albanian, Bulgarian, German, Hungarian, Romanian, Slovak and Turkish—are used in distinct regions of the nation. Some districts are startlingly polyglot. In Prizren, Kosovo, the street signs are printed in three languages—Albanian, Serbo-Croatian and Turkish. And in the Istrian town of Novigrad (also signposted Cittanova) the signs are in Serbo-Croatian and Italian.

English is ever more widely understood in Yugoslavia, though German and Italian prove more useful along the coast. The Berlitz phrase book, *Serbo-Croatian for Travellers,* covers almost all the situations you're likely to encounter in your travels in Yugoslavia.

The Cyrillic alphabet may seem confusing at first, but persevere. You'll soon be able to decipher it with the help of the chart below. The column at left shows the printed capital and small letters; written letters are given in the centre. The third column shows the corresponding letters in the Latin alphabet. And at right you'll find an English word containing the approximate sound.

А а	*А а*	**a**	c**a**r
Б б	*Б б*	**b**	**b**rother
Ц ц	*Ц ц*	**c**	ca**ts**
Ч ч	*Ч ч*	**č**	**ch**urch
Ћ ћ	*Ћ ћ*	**ć**	crun**chi**er
Д д	*Д д*	**d**	**d**own
Џ џ	*Џ џ*	**dž**	**J**une
Ђ ђ	*Ђ ђ*	**dj** or **đ**	see**di**er
Е е	*Е е*	**e**	g**e**t
Ф ф	*Ф ф*	**f**	**f**ather
Г г	*Г г*	**g**	**g**o
Х х	*Х х*	**h**	**h**ouse
И и	*И и*	**i**	m**ee**t
Ј ј	*Ј ј*	**j**	**y**oke
К к	*К к*	**k**	**k**ey
Л л	*Л л*	**l**	**l**ip
Љ љ	*Љ љ*	**lj**	fai**lu**re
М м	*М м*	**m**	**m**outh
Н н	*Н н*	**n**	**n**ot
Њ њ	*Њ њ*	**nj**	o**ni**on
О о	*О о*	**o**	h**o**t
П п	*П п*	**p**	**p**ut
Р р	*Р р*	**r**	**r**ope
С с	*С с*	**s**	**s**ister
Ш ш	*Ш ш*	**š**	**sh**ip
Т т	*Т т*	**t**	**t**op
У у	*У у*	**u**	b**oo**m
В в	*В в*	**v**	**v**ery
З з	*З з*	**z**	**z**ip
Ж ж	*Ж ж*	**ž**	plea**s**ure

Does anyone here speak English?	**Da li neko ovde govori engleski?**

LOST PROPERTY

Many towns have lost-and-found bureaus, but it may be easier to start your inquiries at your hotel or the nearest tourist office. Then report the loss to the *milicija* (police).

In the case of lost children, hotel personnel are in the best position to help with sympathy and knowledgeable action.

Where's the lost property office?	**Gde je biro za nadjene stvari?**
I've lost my wallet.	**Izgubio sam novčanik [lisnicu].**
I've lost my handbag.	**Izgubila sam tašnu.**

MAPS *(plan [karta])*   M

Yugoslavian National Tourist Offices in many countries supply free maps pinpointing resort areas and scenic and historic sights.

On the spot, some local tourist offices give away maps. Bookshops sell maps big and small for visitors in need of greater detail. And newsstands often stock town plans along with the postcards.

The maps in this book were prepared by Falk-Verlag, Hamburg.

a street plan	**plan grada**
a road map of this region	**karta cesta [puteva] ovoga kraja**

MEETING PEOPLE

In the resorts the obvious place to make friends is the beach—the focus for daytime leisure. Alternatively, you can try the *korzo*, the traditional community promenade held daily towards sunset. Most of the precepts for getting to know people anywhere apply to Yugoslavia—be friendly, be yourself, be reasonable.

If a Yugoslav offers you a drink, it's just about obligatory to accept, though there's no stigma attached if you change the subject from brandy to coffee. You are not expected to stand the next round; the hospitality can be returned at a later date.

Handshaking, seemingly at every opportunity, is essential when greeting almost anybody. All this old-fashioned central European courtesy is suddenly forgotten, however, in less-relaxed situations—when clambering aboard an overcrowded bus, for example. *Izvinite* (excuse me) is about all one can say.

As for flirtation possibilities, the situation is as relaxed as anywhere else in Europe, except for those southern areas of Yugoslavia with an oriental cast. Also beware of small towns, where people are more conservative than in cities and tourist-trampled zones.

In Yugoslavia, as elsewhere, always ask permission before taking photos of people.

MONEY MATTERS

Currency *(valuta)*. For currency restrictions, see CUSTOMS AND ENTRY REGULATIONS. The Yugoslavian currency is the dinar (abbreviated *din.*), sometimes called the new dinar (equal to 100 old dinars). Because many people still think in old dinars, you may be bemused to hear prices quoted in seemingly outrageous numbers. Thus 600 new dinars is sometimes called 60,000 (old) dinars or, simply and most confusingly, 60.

Coins: 1, 2, 5, 10, 50, 100 dinars.

Banknotes: 10, 20, 50, 100, 500, 1,000, 5,000 and 20,000 dinars.

Banks and currency exchange offices *(banka; menjačnica)*. Whether you change your money at a bank or an exchange office the rates are identical. But traveller's cheques command a slightly higher exchange rate than cash.

When banks are closed—or crowded or far away—you can change money in any authorized currency exchange office including travel agencies and hotels. Though currency exchange operations may close for a couple of hours at lunchtime they usually remain open until early evening.

Try to assess how much cash you will need in dinars so you don't exchange too much hard currency. Dinars cannot be reconverted before you leave Yugoslavia and only a small amount can be exported. All you can do with unspent dinars at the end of your holiday is pay the airport departure tax and buy Yugoslavian handicrafts in the duty-free shop.

Credit cards *(creditna karta)*. Although many hotels, restaurants and tourist-oriented enterprises accept credit cards, they are less well known beyond the main towns and resorts.

Traveller's cheques *(putni ček)* may be changed at banks, hotels and travel agencies and are also accepted in many shops and restaurants. You'll almost certainly be asked to show your passport when cashing a cheque.

I want to change some pounds/ dollars.	**Želim da promenim funte/ dolare.**
Do you accept traveller's cheques?	**Da li primate putne čekove?**
Can I pay with this credit card?	**Mogu li da platim kreditnom kartom?**

232

NEWSPAPERS AND MAGAZINES *(novine; časopis)*

Most leading western European newspapers, including British dailies and the American *International Herald Tribune* edited in Paris, are sold at major resorts and in a few big cities. The papers usually arrive the day after publication. Popular foreign magazines are also widely available.

Do you have any English-language newspapers?	**Imate li novine na engleskom?**

PACKING

Leave room in your luggage for the souvenirs you'll be buying in Yugoslavia. If you forget to pack a particular item of clothing, it can be easily replaced in any Yugoslavian city or resort. But certain other things may be harder to find—for instance, specific medicines, or gadgets. If you require holiday reading matter, bring along a paperback or two; there's little variety in the English books on sale locally. Some finicky coffee and tea drinkers carry their own supplies. And you might want to invest in a universal bathtub plug; they sometimes go missing in hotels.

PHOTOGRAPHY

You can buy film everywhere in Yugoslavia, but to be sure of your favourite brand, and to save on the cost, bring your own supply from home. Photo shops in cities and small towns alike advertise speedy developing.

In certain areas—generally near military installations, power plants and national borders—photography is forbidden. This is clearly announced by signs showing the silhouette of an old bellows camera circled in red or crossed out with a diagonal red line. (In addition, certain sensitive zones are off limits to foreigners with or without cameras; these are marked with "no entry" or "no stopping for foreigners" signs printed in six languages.)

The quaintly costumed people you may come across are usually quite accustomed to tourists with cameras. However, if you detect any embarrassment or annoyance, the decent course is to desist. One snapshot is scarcely worth an international incident. And more extrovert subjects are probably ready to be filmed around the next bend in the road. Note: when you take someone's picture, never give a tip.

Beware of unusual light conditions, especially the blinding reflections from the sea and white buildings. You may not be able to rely on the electric eye of your automatic camera. Instead use a faster shutter speed to compensate for the glare.

I'd like a film for this camera.	Želim film za ovu kameru.
a black-and-white film	crno-beli film
a colour film	u boji [kolor] film
a colour-slide film	film za kolor dijapozitive
35-mm film	trideset pet milimetara film

POLICE *(milicija)*

The national police, wearing blue uniforms (white in summer), maintain public order and control traffic. Each officer's identity is revealed by his service number, clearly engraved on his belt buckle. Police cars, blue and white, are marked *Milicija* or one of the local linguistic variations.

Where's the nearest police station?	Gde je najbliža milicijska stanica?

PRICES

Inflation in Yugoslavia rages so fiercely that prudent merchants write their price tags in pencil. And the dinar dwindles against foreign currencies almost as fast as the bankers can fix the charts in their windows. Thus the following typical prices are the merest approximation, and expressed in the less volatile terms of U.S. dollars or German marks.

Camping. U.S. $3.50 per person per night, $1.30 for tent or car, $2 per caravan (trailer).

Car hire. *Renault 4* U.S. $17 per day, 17¢ per km., $281 per week with unlimited mileage. *VW Golf* $31 per day, 31¢ per km., $511 per week unlimited mileage. *Opel Kadett* $48 per day, 48¢ per km., or $789 weekly unlimited mileage. Add 15% tax.

Entertainment. Discotheque DM1.50, cinema DM1, symphony concert DM3–6.50, folklore performance DM3–6.50.

Hairdressers. *Woman's* shampoo and blow-dry DM10.50, permanent wave DM10.50. *Man's* haircut DM2.

Hotels (double room with breakfast). De luxe US$60-130, Class A US$32-$100, Class B $19-$58, Class C $16-$44

Meals and drinks. Lunch/dinner (fairly good establishment) DM20, coffee DM1. Yugoslav brandy and most Yugoslav drinks DM1.50, litre of local wine DM6—8, soft drinks DM1.50.

How much is the admission charge?	**Koliko staje ulaz?**
Do you have something cheaper?	**Imate li nešto jevtinije?**
It's too much.	**Suviše je skupo.**

PUBLIC HOLIDAYS *(državni praznik)*

Jan. 1, 2	*Nova godina*	New Year
May 1, 2	*Prvi maj*	Labour Days
July 4	*Dan borca*	Veterans' Day
Nov. 29, 30	*Dan Republike*	Republic Days

In addition, individual republics celebrate a number of their own legal holidays, mostly patriotic.

Are you open tomorrow?	**Da li je otvoreno sutra?**

RADIO AND TV *(radio; televizija)* R

Radio Yugoslavia and regional stations around the country broadcast daily programmes for foreign tourists in ten languages on medium wave and FM. If you have a short-wave set you can tune in to the programmes of the BBC and Voice of America.

Each republic and province has its own television centre. In most places you can pick up two Yugoslavian channels, and near the borders foreign stations as well. Feature films are always shown with the original sound-track and subtitles. Some luxury hotels pipe in foreign TV programmes in English, German, Italian and French or offer feature films on video in various languages.

RELIGIOUS SERVICES

About 50 different churches and religious communities are active in Yugoslavia. Along much of the Adriatic coast and in Slovenia the people are predominantly Roman Catholic, and mass is said daily in churches in many cities and towns. Yugoslavia has relatively few

Protestant churches, mostly in the cities. There are Orthodox churches throughout Serbia, Montenegro and Macedonia, as well as Bosnia-Hercegovina. Most of the mosques are found in Bosnia-Hercegovina, Macedonia and Kosovo. Several towns have historic synagogues.

What time is mass/the service?	U koliko sati je misa/služba?
church	crkva
synagogue	sinagoga
mosque	džamija

RESTAURANTS

Yugoslavs eat well, but at what you may consider eccentric hours. Most people gulp coffee at dawn, for work starts as early as 7 a.m. They take a snack break—breakfast, actually—at around 10 a.m. They finish work at 2 p.m. and have a late, leisurely lunch. Consequently, the dinner hour doesn't begin until 8 or 9 p.m. This explains why restaurants can seem extraordinarily quiet at what tourists take to be normal meal times.

You'll probably breakfast in your hotel; in most cases it's included in the price of the room. Hotel breakfasts range from a spartan continental nibble to a generous hot-and-cold buffet that may eclipse lunch. Or you can have a pastry-and-coffee breakfast in any café.

Restaurants in Yugoslavia come in ten or more varieties, each with a name and its own characteristics. Among them:

Bife. This is how the Yugoslavs write *buffet*—a snack-bar where you may order a light, cheap meal.

Ekspres restoran. An inexpensive self-service restaurant with a limited menu. A bit short on atmosphere as a rule.

Kafana. A pastry-and-snack coffee shop; alcoholic drinks also sold here.

Gostiona. A village inn, often privately owned, with wholesome, home-cooked food.

Restoran. Just about any restaurant, from the humble to the elegant.

Mlečni restoran. A dairy restaurant featuring light meals, pancakes and pastry.

Riblji restoran. Specializing in seafood, but not to the exclusion of meat dishes.

A service charge, usually 10%, is added to restaurant bills. If the service was good, leave a tip of about 10% of the bill.

To help you order...

Could we have a table?	**Možemo li dobito sto?**
Do you have a set menu?	**Da li imate meni?**
I'd like a/an/some...	**Molim Vas...**

beer	**pivo**	*menu*	**jelovnik**
bread	**kruh [hleb]**	*sandwich*	**sendvič**
coffee	**kavu**	*soup*	**juhu**
fish	**ribu**	*tea*	**čaj**
meat	**meso**	*(iced) water*	**vodu (sa ledom)**

... and read the menu

barbun	*red mullet*	**maslac**	*butter*
beli luk	*garlic*	**mleko**	*milk*
biftek	*beefsteak*	**na roštilju**	*grilled*
čokolada	*chocolate*	**pečenje**	*roast*
ćufte	*meatballs*	**perad [živina]**	*fowl*
gljive	*mushrooms*	**piletina**	*chicken*
grožđje	*grapes*	**pršut**	*smoked ham*
jagnjetina	*lamb*	**ragu**	*stew*
jaja	*eggs*	**riža**	*rice*
jastog	*lobster*	**sir**	*cheese*
kobasice	*sausages*	**sladoled**	*ice-cream*
kompot	*stewed fruit*	**šunka**	*ham*
krompir	*potatoes*	**teletina**	*veal*
lignje [kalamari]	*squid*	**variva [zelenje]**	*vegetables*
luk	*onion*	**vino**	*wine*

TIME DIFFERENCES T

Like most of the Continent, Yugoslavia adheres to Central European Time (GMT + 1). In summer the clock is put ahead one hour (GMT + 2).

Los Angeles	Chicago	New York	London	Belgrade
11 a.m.	1 p.m.	2 p.m.	7 p.m.	8 p.m.

What time is it?	**Koliko je sati?**

TIPPING

When in doubt, 10% is a reasonable figure for a tip. Hotel bills are all-inclusive. Though restaurant bills usually feature a 10% service charge, it is customary to tip the waiter up to 10%. Other recommendations: tip the barber or hairdresser 10%; the lavatory attendant a few hundred dinars; the hotel maid a few thousand dinars per week; the tour guide 5 to 10%; tip porters at hotels, airports and railway stations several hundred dinars; round up the fare for the taxi driver (optional).

TOILETS

Much of Yugoslavia preserves reminders of the centuries of Turkish rule, among them the seatless squat toilets you'll find in public conveniences and country restaurants and cafés. But hotels and restaurants serving foreigners normally have western-style facilities.

The pertinent doors are usually marked by symbols—often a silhouetted high-heeled shoe for women and a flat shoe for men—rather than words (*muški* for men and *ženski* for women). In public toilets cubicle doors almost never have locks or latches. The cleaning lady may look in at any time. Be sure to tip her on your way out of her domain.

Where are the toilets?	**Gde je VC** (pronounced *ve-tse*), **molim Vas?**

TOURIST INFORMATION OFFICES *(turistički biro)*

In major cities of Europe and America, Yugoslavian National Tourist Offices offer complete information to help you plan your holiday. They can supply maps, leaflets and brochures on general or specialized subjects about Yugoslavia. They'll also let you consult master directories of hotels and campsites throughout the country, listing all facilities and rates. Among the addresses:

Great Britain: 143 Regent St., London W.1; tel. (01) 734-5243

U.S.A. and Canada: Suite 210, Rockefeller Center, 630 5th Ave., New York, N.Y. 10020; tel. (212) 757-2801

Once on the spot you'll find local tourist information offices in virtually all the towns and resorts. Travel agency offices also stand ready to answer your questions and help you find accommodation.

TRANSPORT

Taxis *(taksi)*. There are plenty of taxis available for hire at ranks in towns and tourist centres. On the whole, fares tend to be rather high. Vehicles are easily recognized. Those in larger towns have meters, but in smaller places, where there may be only one taxi, agree on the fare in advance. Extra charges are levied for luggage and night travel.

Bus services *(autobus)*. Local and long-distance bus service is inexpensive and well developed, particularly along the Adriatic coast, where the most modern equipment is used. During the tourist season, though, the buses can become quite crowded. You can buy tickets in advance at bus stations in the major towns, and for local buses at newsstands and kiosks. Most urban buses are stretched models with accordion pleats in the middle, accommodating swarms of passengers.

Trams/streetcars *(tramvaj)*. The big cities generally have very good, modern tram networks. Service is fast, efficient and cheap. Tickets are sold at newsstands; punch your ticket yourself when you board.

Trains *(vlak [voz])*. The rail network has shrunk in recent years, but the surviving lines have been improved. The most appealing train journey for tourists is the route linking Belgrade with the Montenegrin coast at Bar, famous for its engineering marvels and spectacular scenery. The priority and speed of a train is indicated by its category—local, inter-city express or international express. In season trains tend to be crowded and slow; it's wise to book seats and sleeping accommodation in advance. You save about one-fourth in second class.

Ferries *(trajekt)* link the Adriatic coast with Italian and Greek ports. All the routes between the Adriatic islands and the mainland of Yugoslavia are listed in a ferry schedule booklet available free from travel agencies and tourist information offices. The timetables are confusing at first: only the departure times are listed, so you have to guess the probable arrival time. For drivers the modern drive-through ferries are very convenient. But older boats, built like assault landing craft, require you to back your car on or off. Relax and follow the directions of the expert deck-hands.

Hydrofoils *(hidrokrilac)* provide rapid transport between Italian and Yugoslavian ports, and between the Adriatic islands and the Yugoslavian mainland.

Airplanes *(avion)*. JAT, the national airline, serves all the coastal and inland airports, big and small. Considering the mountainous terrain and the state of the roads, you may choose flying as the efficient way of crossing the country.

Where can I get a taxi?	**Gde mogu da dobijem taksi?**
When's the next bus to...?	**Kad ide sledeći autobus za...?**
single (one way)	**u jednom pravcu**
return (roundtrip)	**povratna karta**
Where's the railway station?	**Gde je železnička stanica?**
Is there a flight to...?	**Da li ima let za...?**

W WATER *(voda)*

Not only can you drink the water, in some areas it's positively delicious right out of the tap. But the change in mineral content may disturb delicate stomachs. If you're sensitive, ask for bottled mineral water (*mineralna voda* or *kisela voda*). It's inexpensive, it tastes good, and, it's claimed, good for what ails you.

a bottle of mineral water	**flaša mineralne vode**
fizzy/carbonated	**gazirane**
still/non-carbonated	**negazirane**
Is this drinking water?	**Da li je ovo voda za piće?**

WEIGHTS AND MEASURES

Yugoslavia uses the metric system. For fluid and distance measures, see page 224.

Temperature

°C	30	25	20	15	10	5	0	5	10	15	20	25	30	35	40	45
°F		-20	-10	0	10	20	30	40	50	60	70	80	90	100	110	

Length

cm	0	5	10	15	20	25	30
inches	0	2	4	6	8	10	12

metres	0	1 m	2 m
ft./yd.	0	1 ft 1 yd.	2 yd.

Weight

grams	0	100	200	300	400	500	600	700	800	900	1 kg
ounces	0	4	8	12	1 lb. 20	24	28	2 lb.			

yes/no	**da/ne**
please/thank you	**molim/hvala**
excuse me/ you're welcome	**izvinite/nema na čemu [molim]**
where/when/how	**gde/kad/kako**
how long/how far	**koliko dugo/koliko daleko**
yesterday/today/tomorrow	**juče/danas/sutra**
day/week/month/year	**dan/nedelja/mesec/godina**
left/right	**levo/desno**
up/down	**gore/dole**
good/bad	**dobro/loše**
big/small	**veliko/malo**
cheap/expensive	**jeftino/skupo**
hot/cold	**vruće/hladno**
old/new	**staro/novo**
open/closed	**otvoreno/zatvoreno**
I'd like...	**Zelim**
How much is that?	**Koliko košta?**
What time is it?	**Koliko je sati?**
What does this mean?	**Šta ovo znači?**
What do you call this?	**Kako se ovo kaše?**
Is there anyone here who speaks English?	**Ima li ovde neko ko govori engleski?**
I don't understand.	**Ne razumem.**
Please speak more slowly.	**Molim Vas govorite sporije.**
Please write it down.	**Molim Vas naspišite mi to.**
Help me, please.	**Pomozite mi, molim Vas.**
Get a doctor—quickly!	**Zovite doktora—brzo!**
What do you want?	**Šta želite?**
Just a minute.	**Samo trenutak.**
Waiter, please.	**Konobar, molim.**

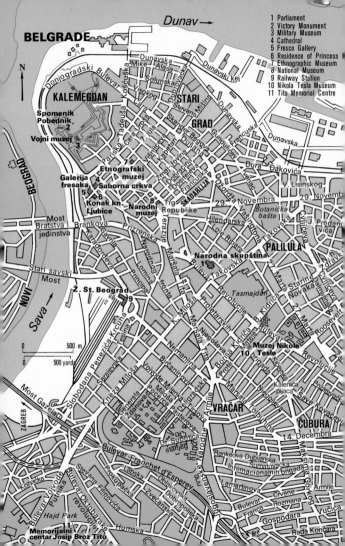

BELGRADE

Dunav →

N

KALEMEGDAN

Spomenik
Pobednik

Vojni muzej

Galerija
fresaka

Konak kn
Ljubice

Etnografski
muzej

Saborna crkva

Narodni
muzej

STARI
GRAD

Dunavska
Mike Alasa
Solunska

SKADARLIJA

Trg
Republike

Dunavski kei

Dunavska

Đakovica

V. Lisinskog

29. Novembra

Botanička
bašta

29. Novembr

PALILULA

Narodna skupština

Most
Bratstva i
jedinstva

BEOGRAD

NOVI

Sava →

Stari savski
Most

Brankova

Ž. St. Beograd

Tasmajdan

Muzej Nikole
Tesle

VRAČAR

ČUBURA

14. Decembra

Most Gazelan

ZAGREB

Hajd Park

Memorijalni
centar Josip Broz Tito

Bulevar Franchet d'Esperey

NIŠ

0   500 m

0   500 yards

1 Parliament
2 Victory Monument
3 Military Museum
4 Cathedral
5 Fresco Gallery
6 Residence of Princess
7 Ethnographic Museum
8 National Museum
9 Railway Station
10 Nikola Tesla Museum
11 Tito Memorial Centre

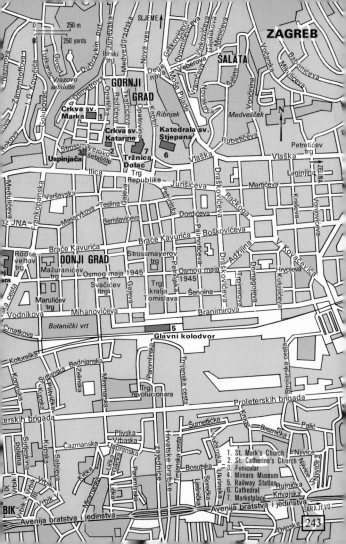

ZAGREB

SLJEME

SALATA

GORNJI GRAD

Crkva sv. Marka 1

Crkva sv. Katarine 2

Uspinjača 3

Tržnica Dolac 7

Katedrala sv. Stjepana 6

Medveščak

Petretićev trg

Vlaška

Laginjina

Ribnjak

Trg Republike

Jurišićeva

Ilica

Varšavska

Teslina

Masarykova

Berislavićeva

Đorđićeva

Braće Kavurića

Boškovićeva

DONJI GRAD

Roose-veltov trg

Mažuranićev trg

Strossmayerov trg

Osmog maja 1945

Osmog maja 1945

Trg kralja Tomislava

Šenoina

Marulićev trg

Svačićev trg

Mihanovićeva

Branimirova

Botanički vrt

5

Glavni kolodvor

Koturaška

Bednjanska

Trg revolucionara

Proleterskih brigada

Palić

Plivska Vrbaska

Čazmanska

Bosutska

BIK

Avenija bratstva i jedinstva

Avenija bratstva i jedinstva

SARAJEVO

1. St. Mark's Church
2. St. Catherine's Church
3. Funicular
4. Mimara Museum
5. Railway Station
6. Cathedral
7. Marketplace

243

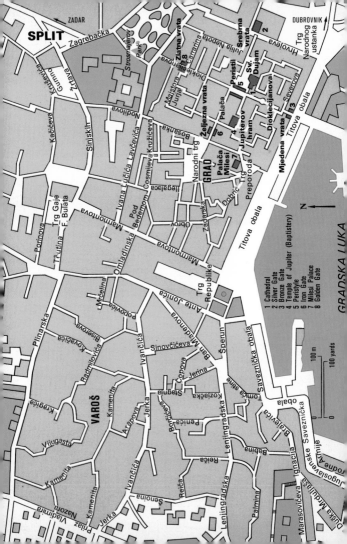

SPLIT

ZADAR

Zagrebačka

DUBROVNIK

Trg Narodnog ustanka

VAROŠ

GRAD

GRADSKA LUKA

Zlatna vrata
Srebrna vrata
Peristil
Sv. Dujam
Palača
Željezna vrata
Jupiterov hram
Palača Milesi
Mjedena vrata

Titova obala

1 Cathedral
2 Silver Gate
3 Bronze Gate
4 Temple of Jupiter (Baptistery)
5 Peristyle
6 Iron Gate
7 Milesi Palace
8 Golden Gate

100 m
100 yards

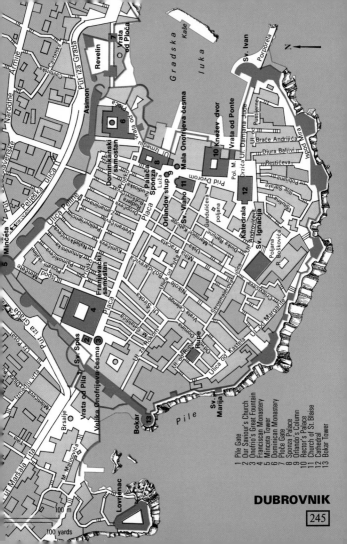

DUBROVNIK

1 Pile Gate
2 Our Saviour's Church
3 Onofrio's Great Fountain
4 Franciscan Monastery
5 Minčeta Tower
6 Dominican Monastery
7 Ploče Gate
8 Sponza Palace
9 Orlando's Column
10 Rector's Palace
11 Church of St. Blaise
12 Cathedral
13 Bokar Tower

100 m
100 yards

endava

Čakovec

Varaždin

Ludbreg

Koprivnica

Nagykanizsa

H U N G A R Y

Pécs

Drava

Križevci

Zelina

Virje

Djurdjevac

Barcs

Vrbovec

Bjelovar

Virovitica

ugo Selo

Čazma

Veliki Zdenci

Ivanić Grad

Ilova

Podrav Slatina

Donji Miholjac

Drava

Popovača

Daruvar

Bizovac

NOVI SAD

Sisak

Kutina

Bijela

Pakrac

Slavonska Požega

Našice

etrinja

Kupa

Novska

Djakovo

jotina

Dubica

Una

Novska

Okučani

Nova Gradiška

Sava

Slavonski Brod

Sava

BEOGRAD

Dvor

Božanska Novi

Prijedor

Kozarak

Ivanjska

Vrbas

Derventa

Bosanski Šamac

Sana

Prnjavor

Ukrina

Gradačac

Sanski Most

Banja Luka

Kotor Varoš

Klupe

Doboj

V. Usora

Bosna

Gračanica

Spreča

Bosanski Petrovac

Ključ

Borostica jezero

Borci

Stenjak

Ozimica

Dolac

Modračko jez.

Titov Drvar

Mrkonjić Grad

Jajce

Žepče

Krivaja

247

B O S N A   i
H E R C E G O V I N A

Travnik

Zenica

SARAJEVO

Olovo

0   25km
0   25 miles

N

DALMATIAN COAST

CONTINENTAL
YUGOSLAVIA

SOUTHERN YUGOSLAVIA

Niš

Bela Palanka

Pirot

Novi Pazar

Dren

Kuršumlija

Prokupije

S R B I J A

Dimitrovgrad

Ibar

Ribariće

Podujevo

Titova Mitrovica

Lebane

Jablanica

Medvedja

Leskovac

Predejane

Vlasinsko jez.

Sitnica

Tulare

Klina

Priština

Manastir Gračanica

KOSOVO

Laplje Selo

Vranje

Bosilegrad

Ribarci

Suva Reka

Zrze

Uroševac

Binačka Morava

Preševo

Bujanovac

Pčinja

Kriva Palanka

Prizren

Vratnika

Kačanik

Kumanovo

Kriva

Kratovo

Skopje

Kočani

Delče

Tetovo

Manastir sveti Pantelejmon

Sv. Nikole

Gostivar

Vardar

Treska

Titov Veles

Štip

Radoviš

A L B A N I A

Mavrovo

Kičevo

Brod

Izvor

M A K E D O N I J A

Negotino

Strumica

Debar

Vardar

Lukovo

Botun

Kruševo

Prilep

Jezero Tikveš

Struga

Sopotnica

Crna Reka

Topolčani

Crna Reka

Gevgelija

Ohrid

Ohridsko jezero

Resen

Bitola

B U G A R S K A

0   25 km

0   25 miles

252

Sveti Naum

Prespansko jezero

G R E E C E

INDEX

An asterisk (*) next to a page number indicates a map reference. Where there is more than one set of page references, the one in bold type refers to the main entry. For index to Practical Information, see pp. 212–13.